To: Lori ♥

From: Julie Miller

Nov. 28th — Thanksgiving '96

May you find comfort & hope
in the pages of this book!

A DAILY DEVOTIONAL

SECRET
STRENGTH

For those who search

JONI EARECKSON TADA

MULTNOMAH BOOKS - SISTERS, OREGON

SECRET STRENGTH
© 1994 by Joni, Inc.

published by Multnomah Books
a part of the Questar publishing family

International Standard Book Number: 0-88070-590-6

Contents based on material that appeared in a previous book entitled *Secret Strength*

Printed in the United States of America

Design by David Uttley

For information:
QUESTAR PUBLISHERS, INC.
POST OFFICE BOX 1720
SISTERS, OREGON 97759

94 95 96 97 98 99 00 01 02 03 — 10 9 8 7 6 5 4 3 2 1

*For
Mom and Dad Tada*

I wish I could remember all the times and the places where I've learned those…unforgettable things. A lingering phrase from someone's long ago sermon that has stuck with me. A poem, a catch phrase, a memorized paragraph that hasn't shaken itself from my mind.

Like you, I read a little here, gather some ideas there, and somehow the Lord weaves these flashes of thoughts into the fabric of my own study of God and His Word. I wish I could exactly recall each author or speaker, pastor or friend from whom I've gleaned so much. I would want, here and now, to give them full acknowledgment and my special thanks .

A few names come immediately to mind—Steve Estes, Elisabeth Elliott, C. S. Lewis, Dr. Martin Lloyd-Jones, Phil Yancey, John MacArthur, Kay Arthur, Bill Gothard, to name a few. I beg the indulgence of others whom I'm regrettably unable to list here. My hope is that if they see the fleeting imprint of their original ideas in my book, they will be pleased that those ideas are having an impact for the Lord Jesus on new and different readers.

I especially want to thank Bev Singleton, our Media Coordinator here at *Joni and Friends* for the years of tirelessly helping me research, write, compile, and organize my radio programs. Also a word of thanks to our friends at Ambassador Advertising Agency who keep giving me deadlines so I can research and write more. For this book I have chosen those radio messages that have touched my heart the most.

Also, I have occasionally drawn from some of my favorite parts of *A Step Further.*

And my lasting thanks remain with Larry Libby, my friend and editor at Multnomah. From him I am learning to slow down, enjoy words, and write with my heart.

*You will
seek Me and find Me,
when you search for Me with
all your heart.*

JEREMIAH 29:13

An Opening Thought

'No eye has seen, no ear has heard,
no mind has conceived what God has prepared for
those who love him'—but God has revealed
it to us by his Spirit.

1 CORINTHIANS 2:9-10, NIV

What's so secret about God?

Nothing. And yet everything.

Early on in my life with Christ I discovered that if I desired a deeper, more intimate knowledge of the Lord, I would be sent on a search. There were treasures to dig. Precious gems to mine.

If you are a believer, you already have everything you need for the journey. You have been initiated into the fellowship of the skies. You have His Word, the key to heaven's hieroglyphics. You have the mind of Christ. Now you must find His heart! He waits, tenderly and compassionately, to reveal Himself to you.

Would you like a little help in your search? Then I invite you, my fellow seeker, to enjoy this book as a companion on your venture. "You will seek me and find me, when you search for me with all your heart" (Jeremiah 29:13).

May you find that secret strength that is His to give and yours to receive.

IN WEAKNESS MADE STRONG

*God chose the weak things of the world
to shame the strong.*

1 CORINTHIANS 1:27, NIV

Just whom does God delight in using to accomplish His plans?

Consider Gideon. Gideon was threshing wheat—crouching in a winepress to avoid detection by Israel's enemy, the Midianites—when the Lord Himself appeared with a message. "The LORD is with you, mighty warrior" (Judges 6:12, NIV).

You can almost visualize Gideon's head popping up out of the winepress. "Er, excuse me? Were you talking to me?" He'd probably been called a lot of things by his friends and family, but never *that*.

Scripture tells us "the LORD turned to him and said, 'Go in the strength you have and save Israel out of Midian's hand. Am I not sending you?'" (6:14).

Gideon, apparently, wasn't aware of *any* strength. He sputtered and stuttered and reminded this Stranger that he was the weakest member of the weakest clan of the weakest tribe in the weak nation of Israel. Definitely no West Point graduate. If God was looking for warrior material, He must have been peering into the wrong winepress.

But no, God wanted Gideon. The task was ridiculously large. The biblical account affirms the enemy soldiers filled a great valley, "thick as locusts. Their camels could no more be counted than the sand on the seashore" (7:12). Yet God accomplished His plans through Gideon's little band of three hundred men, "in order that Israel may not boast against me that her own strength has saved her" (7:2).

Perhaps you feel a bit like Gideon today. Your gifts aren't many. Your talents are few. Like Gideon, you have to admit you're not the brightest or strongest member of your own family.

Take a look, my weak friends, at 1 Corinthians 1:26-29. Start chasing this theme through the pages of your Bible and you'll be at it for months! It pleased God to pick the unlikely, unlovely, and unheralded to get His job done. He picked weak and ordinary me. He's even picked you...with all your weakness and inadequacy, in spite of your mistakes and fumbled opportunities.

Then, when the task is completed and God's work has been accomplished through your life, guess who gets the glory?

STRONGHOLD

Read 1 Corinthians 2:1-5. Take heart knowing that if God did such great things through a man who often trembled in weakness and fear, He can surely use you!

HURRICANE WARNING

*I will trust in the shelter of
Your wings.*
PSALM 61:4, NKJV

When Hurricane Diana slammed into the Carolina coastline a few years ago, the networks were there with cameras rolling. We watched wide eyed as 100-mile-per-hour winds overturned cars, drove pleasure craft into beach house bedrooms, and even bent streetlights in half.

But out of all of those televised scenes of Diana's wrath, one image lingers in my mind. On a dark back street, one lone man in a yellow slicker clung to a telephone pole as torrents of rain and a screaming wind sought to hurl him backwards into the darkness.

I've returned to that mental snapshot a number of times in the intervening years. I think of it as I come across verses in the Bible that speak of how absolutely weak we really are—mentally, physically, and spiritually. God keeps bringing home the fact that we *dare not* trust ourselves to find or follow the right road.

For that very reason, God also spends a great deal of time in His Word reminding us how strong, secure, and dependable He really is. Who has said it better than David in Psalm 61?

Some have suggested this psalm was composed when David was driven from his throne and from Jerusalem during the rebellion of his son Absalom. It may have been the darkest day in the king's tumultuous life. He was faced with the humiliation of a successful coup that overthrew his leadership, as well as with the defection of some of his closest friends and most trusted aides—all at the instigation of his own dearly loved son.

How did David feel? Psalm 61:2 says his heart was *overwhelmed*. The dark winds of adversity and sorrow had never blown so hard.

What did he pray? "Lead me to the rock that is higher than I." God, this is over my head! I'm absolutely drowning. I need a Rock I can hang onto before I go under, a Tower of Refuge where I can hide and find rest.

God at times exposes us to the raw forces of the real world. Assaulted by a barrage of heartaches and hardships, we are overwhelmed with a sense of our own inadequacy—our moral and mental weakness. When that happens, we are driven to cling to Him all the more closely, aren't we? We learn the same lesson as that man in the yellow slicker. Find the best refuge, the strongest rock, the firmest and most unshakable defense and *hold on with all your heart*. As though your very life depended on it.

STRONGHOLD

The next time you see a storm brewing in your life, hang on to these "telephone poles": Deuteronomy 4:29-31; Psalm 8:1-3; Psalm 61:2-4; Matthew 7:24-27.

FLEXIBILITY

I have learned to be content
in whatever circumstances I am.

PHILIPPIANS 4:11

A good friend of mine, injured only a short while ago, is still going through all the painful adjustments of life in a wheelchair. Even though she's loaded with beauty and brains, that doesn't make coping with the problems of her disability any easier.

I'll admit, right along with her, that it's tough finding slacks which hang just right when you're sitting down. It's hard finding clothes that fit well when you're always having to be reaching and pulling and pushing in your wheelchair. It's a difficult thing to have other people do your makeup or comb your hair just right.

For instance, there are five different women who on various days help me go through my morning routine. On Monday, my hairstyle is an original creation by Irene. On Tuesday it has the Judy touch. On Wednesday it features the Beverly bouffant, and on Thursday Francie gives it a special flair. On Friday I come to work with a Lynda look.

Now, to be sure, I wear my hair basically the same way every day. But you can't expect five different women to artfully handle a brush and comb in exactly the same way you might want to do it yourself. Obviously, some things are just going to be done a little differently.

But one thing I've been able to tell my friend in her

adjustments is that a disability can really teach you how to be *flexible*. We know, for instance, that Paul had a disability. Yet he didn't always insist on having things exactly his own way. He wasn't picky.

In a letter to friends at Philippi, the battered apostle revealed his "secret"—doing all things through Him. There's something commendable in that approach to life. There are simply some things—whatever our disability or life situation might be—about which we need to be flexible.

Leaning on the strength of his Lord, Paul learned to be satisfied. With an empty stomach or a full one. In days of health or when he had to depend on others in his disability. In the comfortable homes of dear Christian friends or deep in the bowels of a Roman dungeon. In Christ, he was flexible. And because of that flexibility, God blessed him with great contentment.

STRONGHOLD

Read Philippians 4:11-13, and then you might want to pray: Help me, Father, to subtract my desires to have things exactly my own way. Forgive me if I keep adding more and more wants, for You know just what I need. And in that I am content.

NO DIFFERENT STORY

And lead us not into temptation.

MATTHEW 6:13, NIV

T
he writer of Hebrews describes Scripture as a sharp sword. From my perspective, it often feels more like a needle. One verse that has needled me for years is 1 Corinthians 10:13: "No temptation has seized you except what is common to man. And God is faithful; he will not let you be tempted beyond what you can bear. But when you are tempted, he will also provide a way out so that you can stand up under it "(NIV).

Why does that verse prick me so? Because every now and then I'm tempted to think that God *couldn't* expect from me what He does from others. Obviously it's a "different story" in my case, right?

I remember lying on my hospital bed years ago, thinking that God was putting me through more than I could take. *Paralysis. Total and permanent.* But then there was good ol' 1 Corinthians 10:13 reminding me that God will not let me be tempted beyond what I can bear.

The verse came back to pierce me again when I was in my late twenties, single, and with every prospect of remaining so. Sometimes lust or a bit of fantasizing would seem so inviting—and so easy to justify. After all, hadn't I already given up more than most Christians just by being disabled? Didn't my wheelchair entitle me to a little slack now and then? Yet the words stared up at me from the pages of my Bible. "God is faithful...He will provide a way out...you can stand up under it."

When God allows you to suffer, do you have the tendency to use your very trials as an excuse for sinning? Or do you feel that since you've given God a little extra lately by taking such abuse, He owes you a "day off"?

I have a hunch we've all experienced this inner battle. But when we sit down and examine our lame protests in the strong light of a verse like 1 Corinthians 10:13, the excuses just fade away, one by one.

God gives me grace to live in a wheelchair which He doesn't give you if you can walk. But He gives you grace to endure an unwanted divorce or the death of a spouse or the loss of your job or the rebellion of a child, which He doesn't give me. God provides the way of escape, the means by which we may bear up under our individual trials.

The question is never, "Can you obey?" It's, "_Will_ you obey?"

STRONGHOLD

First Corinthians 10:13 is good, but go a step further and start reading from the very first verse in chapter 10. How are the examples of Moses and his followers a warning to you? See also Romans 16:25-27 and Hebrews 5:7-9.

LINES OF COMMUNICATION

*Do you not know that your bodies are
members of Christ?*

1 CORINTHIANS 6:15

A little boy stood by my wheelchair, poked my knee and insisted, "You can make your leg move; just try!"

"But I am trying," I chuckled.

"No, you're just not thinking hard enough."

There was no way I could convince this boy. I attempted to explain that although I had great ideas in my head, it was of no use. I could give all the commands I wanted, but if the lines of communication were down, there was no way my legs and arms were going to respond.

Paul used the analogy of head and body to illustrate our relationship with Christ in Colossians 2:19. A healthy spiritual body of believers takes its direction from Christ, the Head. Jesus gives us instruction through His Word. We, His body, trust and obey, responding in prayer.

But what happens when those communication lines break down? The person who refuses to trust and obey damages the lines of communication between himself and God. Actually, the Bible underscores that almost verbatim in Colossians 2:18.

I think my own body is the best visual aid. My head, you see, has a whole lot of great plans and dreams for my hands and my legs. Unfortunately, my body refuses to listen. My spinal cord injury severed the communication lines between my head and my hands and feet. As a result, all of those fine plans and ideas simply remain in my mind. Personally, I think my body's really missing out.

Is it all that different a situation from the spiritual condition of many believers today? Our Head, Christ, has some grand things in store for us—good ideas that He would love us to carry out, using you and me, His hands and legs down here on earth. But sad to say, our communication lines are often damaged, and God's Word isn't getting through. We don't trust or obey. We don't respond in prayer.

The result? Well, a body like mine. Numb and useless. Or weak and frail, at best.

Are your lines of communication open today? Listen to God's Word. Pray in return. Keep spiritually healthy. To paraphrase that little boy, you *can* make the right moves...if you try.

STRONGHOLD

To test those lines of communication, begin with Matthew 6:5-13. What inspires—or convicts—you most about this Scripture? The lines are open, so make sure you use them this week.

CLAY AND WAX

*Humble yourselves, therefore, under the
mighty hand of God.*

1 PETER 5:6

I recall visiting a sculptor's studio. She was working on several designs, large lumps of clay, covered with damp cheesecloth. The clay could readily harden if the humidity or temperature in her studio changed even slightly.

But not so with the wax my sculptor friend used in designing pieces for reproduction. It remained soft and pliable, easy to work with. Whenever she wanted to create a work of art, she would warm the wax with a hair dryer and it was immediately ready.

Hardened clay is brittle. If dropped, it can fracture into a thousand pieces. Dropped wax, however, only bends from the pressure of the fall and can be quickly remolded.

People are like that. People who are hardened in their resolve against God are brittle; their emotions are easily damaged. But those who bend to the will of God find perfect expression in however God molds them.

I thought of these things some time back when I was in bed, depressed, as a result of a pressure sore. For three months I struggled to remain pliable and open to God's will. In one of those mad, midnight moments during my long convalescence, teetering between a hardened clay and a melted wax response, I came up with a song.

I have a piece of china, a pretty porcelain vase
It holds such lovely flowers, captures everyone's gaze
But fragile things do slip and fall as everybody knows
And when my days came crashing down, my tears
    began to flow.

But don't we all cry when pretty things get broken,
Don't we all cry at such an awful loss?
But Jesus will dry your tears as He has spoken
'Cause He was the one broken on the cross.

My life was just like china, a lovely thing to me
Full of porcelain promises of all that I might be.
But fragile things do slip and fall as everybody knows
And when my vase came crashing down, my tears
    began to flow.

But Jesus is no porcelain prince, His promises won't
    break
His holy Word holds fast and sure, His love no one can
    shake.
So if your life is shattered by sorrow, pain, or sin
His healing love will reach right down and make you
    whole again.

STRONGHOLD

*Read 1 Peter 4:12-19; 5:6-11 and let the words soften your
will to the shaping of the Master's hand.*

Rejoice in your suffering!

DIRTY LAUNDRY

*God has chosen the foolish things of
the world to shame the wise.*

1 CORINTHIANS 1:27

None of us would like to hang out our dirty laundry for public view. Those ugly stains, embarrassing blotches, smears, and smudges are for our eyes only.

We sometimes feel the same way as believers. We catch ourselves hanging out a "laundered" version of the Christian life to attract unbelievers into our fold. We play down the problems, throw a cover over the trials and tragedies, and push all our weak or wounded brothers and sisters to the rear. We don't want anyone thinking, "Look how this so-called loving God treats His devoted followers." And we certainly don't want the handicaps, heartaches, divorces, and dissensions in our church to be ugly smears against God's good name.

It's strange when you consider that our Lord Jesus did not seek to avoid the embarrassing blotches of His society. He actually sought out the company of prostitutes, outcasts, and indigents, apparently fearing no harm to God's reputation. While studiously avoiding the crisply laundered Pharisees, Jesus didn't seem embarrassed to hang around, or for that matter, hang out, the dirty laundry.

There was this difference, however. The most obvious way God used suffering to glorify Himself back then was to miraculously *remove* it. Jesus went about restoring sight to the blind, healing the lepers, raising the dead—doing all sorts of awesome things to ease human misery. And sure enough, even when unbelievers and scoffers saw the miracles, they marveled and glorified God.

Today, God has another way of using suffering to glorify Himself. Strange as it may seem, God often not only allows but actually ensures that you and I, His children, undergo and endure long periods of difficulty, pain, and struggle. If you and I enjoyed nothing but ease and comfort, our world would never learn anything very impressive about God. It would never learn that our God is *worth* serving—even when the going gets tough.

So let unbelievers see what God is doing in your life. Don't hide your heartaches and struggles, hypocritically pretending they don't exist. Instead, concentrate on staying loyal to your God in the midst of them.

It may be the most convincing argument your neighbors ever see or hear about the God you love.

STRONGHOLD

Look at what Paul says in 1 Corinthians 1:26-29. How can you see yourself in this portion of Scripture? How might you reach out to those believers who are in pain or are embarrassed by failure?

COMING GLORY

*We look not at the things which are seen, but
at the things which are not seen.*

2 CORINTHIANS 4:18

A *t some point in his dramatic rise to prominence,
he took a fork in the road. And never looked
back.... And though he was a young man, hardly
into his prime, he began to talk more and more about
death...his death.*

Jesus' disciples must have been blown away.
Bewildered. Even Peter, one of the privileged inner circle,
tried to stop all the illogical talk about betrayal, humiliation, and death. He was stunned when the Teacher turned
on him with a harsh reprimand (Matthew 16:23).

Jesus would have no more political agendas pushed on
Him. From then on, He would clarify the agenda of His
Father. At the same time, however, the Lord was aware
that His men were bruised and shaken over the turn of
events. They needed encouragement. So after six more
days of talk about "denying yourself" and "taking up your
cross" and "losing your life to find it," the Lord did something amazing for them which has become known as the
transfiguration of Christ (Matthew 17:1-3, 5-8).

What an uplift that must have been to those men, so
down at heart over all the talk of death. Up on that hill-
top, Christ helped them to see *beyond* the cross...into the
splendor of the resurrection.

Yes, there would be suffering—unspeakable agony—
ahead.

But after that…glory.

Can you and I hold onto that thought in the middle of our deepest heartaches…when we are most bewildered and perplexed…when life seems heavy, almost unendurable? Can we remember that glory is coming? That we, too, are being transfigured?

There are times when our Lord must long for us to look beyond the heaviness of our circumstances and catch a glimpse of the splendor and glory to come. Eternity lies ahead—really just a few steps down the path. What's more, the transforming might of the resurrected Christ is at work in your life *today,* this very moment, shaping you into a mature man or godly woman. Changing you to resemble Him.

There's something glorious coming. It's already breaking across the horizon…I can see it in your face.

STRONGHOLD

If you're hurting right now, hold on to the thoughts expressed in 2 Corinthians 4:11-18. What reasons does Paul offer for not losing heart in our daily struggles? Look closer at verses 16-18. What is Paul's counsel? Take a few moments right now to "fix your eyes" on the Lord Jesus.

V17 For our light & momentary troubles are achieving for us an eternal glory that far outweighs them all V18 So we fix our eyes not on what is seen, but what is unseen. For what is seen is temporary, but what is unseen is eternal.

PARTAKERS OF CHRIST

For we have become partakers of Christ.
HEBREWS 3:14

I remember her name, her face, and where she went for first-period class. Donna Rutley was a senior when I was a lowly freshman. Donna was a Christian and everybody knew it and admired her for it. She was involved in high school clubs, student government, and sports, and to me she moved through the halls with her feet inches above the floor. The classic blonde-haired, blue-eyed beauty seemed oblivious to her good looks, choosing not to spend her break times primping in front of the girls' room mirror but instead reaching out to new kids like me.

I studied her. Admired her. Mimicked her mannerisms and copied her style. I tried hard to be a miniature Donna Rutley.

Long after she graduated, when I was a senior, I realized something. I never got to know Donna Rutley. I knew *about* her. We'd rarely talked. I knew nothing of her home and family, goals and dreams. Though I "worshiped her from afar" she stepped out of my life, completely and permanently. Yet thinking back on that memory, Donna Rutley taught me a spiritual lesson I'll never forget.

It's not enough to do our best to be like Christ. The writer of Hebrews tells us that we "have become partakers of Christ," and should be "partakers of His holiness"

(Hebrews 3:14, 12:10, KJV). Peter tells us that through God's promises we can be partakers of His divine nature (2 Peter 1:4).

The sufferings we encounter in life—even garden-variety sorts of trials—are meant to *help* us partake of Christ. For when we enter the fellowship of His sufferings, God strips us of our "self-help" mindset. We are forced to our knees and driven to lean on His grace. Then—and it seems only then—can God impart His Son's character to us. In so doing, we are "made like Him."

No, *we* don't build up Christ's character in our own lives. He takes responsibility for building us when we become partakers of Him. Only when I partake of Him, when I share in His life, read His Word, abide in His presence, converse with Him in prayer, seek His counsel, and delight in His fellowship do I become more like Christ...even in my sufferings.

Wherever you are, Donna Rutley, thanks for the lesson.

STRONGHOLD

Do you long to know Christ? Or do you only know about *Him? Take a look at Philippians 3:7-11. When Paul says in verse 10 that he wants to know Christ, what does his desire also include? How can you be "like Him in His death"?*

BEATING THE WAVES

The righteous runs into it and is safe.

PROVERBS 18:10

I 've always loved the ocean. I treasure special memories of camping at Bethany Beach in Delaware when I was a girl. The waves would come in over a long sandbar, breaking up to seven feet high, spilling creamy surf over acres of sand.

Now, to a child of six or seven those waves looked pretty high. When I saw them coming, my first inclination was to swim the other way. But that was a mistake, because the rolling, foaming surf would toss you every which way, sometimes holding you underneath the water for what seemed to be forever.

No, I learned young the best thing to do when those waves swelled was to swim fast *toward* them and dive *under* them before they had a chance to break on top of you. You really had to hold your breath as you dove through the wave. But, oh, the relief you felt as you broke the surface and could hear that huge wave breaking behind you. *You had beat the wave,* and it was exhilarating.

Funny how the lessons you learn at a young age stick with you through the years. Because even though I don't dive or swim anymore, I still feel like I can "beat the waves."

Waves of crisis or difficulty roll in from the horizon

and threaten to break over my life. Looking up at them, they seem so high, so insurmountable. My first inclination is to run the other way from those frightening problems. But I've learned that there is no fast escape. Running from problems only tosses me in a foaming fury of entanglements and frustrations and emotions later on.

Jonah learned that lesson in a tough college course called Obedience 101. When he tried to run from the clear challenge God had laid before him, life became exceedingly complicated. In the inhospitable confines of a fish's belly, the reluctant prophet reflected on his attempted escape (see Jonah 2:3, 5).

Jonah would agree with me that the best way to beat those waves of trials and tough challenges is to *face* them. Head on. Almost anticipating them. Sometimes I find myself literally diving into the middle of a problem before it has a chance to crash on top of me.

And when by God's grace I come through it all? Oh, the relief of knowing that problem is behind me. With God's help, I've beaten it. What an invigorating feeling!

And if only I could swim…I think I could still beat those waves!

STRONGHOLD

When problems are about to break on top of you, what will help you stand your ground? Look at the first three sentences in James 4:7-8. Underline the verb of action in each sentence and make a commitment today to face your problems with that advice in mind.

Submit
Resist
Come near
Wash
Purify

COMPETENT TO COMFORT

*We can comfort those in any trouble with the comfort
we ourselves have received from God.*

2 CORINTHIANS 1:4, NIV

When you think of comforting someone, what comes to your mind? An arm around a friend's shoulder? A hug for a child with a scraped knee? An encouraging note in the mail? Perhaps you picture yourself at a neighbor's kitchen table with a cup of coffee, a listening ear, and a handy tissue. It's almost a pleasant picture, isn't it?

But can you picture yourself comforting a belligerent alcoholic who's trying to kick the habit? Or a cousin who's raging because she's just learned she has multiple sclerosis? Or a teen who's deeply depressed over a poor self-image? Or a forty-year-old executive who's just gone through bankruptcy? Or a young woman who has just been sentenced to prison? Or a grieving parent with a homosexual son?

Perhaps we'd like to help but feel that "somebody else" would be, well, better qualified. There must be others, we tell ourselves, who will move into that situation and know what to say or do. We reason that our experience has only prepared us for comforting another in a similar situation.

Be careful about letting yourself off the hook with those thoughts. God's Word seems to indicate something else. In his second letter to the Corinthians, Paul doesn't say we can only comfort those with whom we can identify—the common dilemmas, the everyday obstacles, the minor bumps and bruises. He says *any* trouble, *any* heartache, disease, or injury.

All too often we feel reluctant, insecure, or anxious when called upon to comfort someone in troubles greater than our own. But God says it's possible. And our rich resource of enabling is the Father of compassion and the God of all comfort. He'll give you the right words to say. Or the wisdom to say none at all. His love will speak through you and His grace will flow out of you.

You don't have to have a degree in sociology. You don't have to be a drug-rehabilitation specialist, family counselor, psychologist, or seminary graduate. And no, you don't have to have survived a divorce to comfort someone else through a divorce. You needn't have lost a child in order to comfort a mother through her miscarriage.

Anyone can demonstrate love to anyone else, and since God comforts us in *all* our troubles, is it asking too much to comfort others in *any* trouble?

STRONGHOLD

Stop right now and put your letter-writing paper and telephone book in clear view as a reminder to write a note of encouragement to someone before the day is done. Read 2 Corinthians 1:3-11 and memorize verses 3-4.

HIGHER SERVICE

Do your work heartily, as for the Lord.
COLOSSIANS 3:23

My husband is the strong, silent type—the picture of a robust, athletic man. Perhaps that's why a few of his racquetball buddies express surprise when they learn Ken is married to a quadriplegic in a wheelchair. "It's really amazing," they say, "that you've given up your life to serve a handicapped woman."

Those sorts of comments aren't uncommon. You hear people talking about the burden of caring for an elderly mother, the sacrifice of serving a sick child or of devoting years to a handicapped youngster. Sometimes people will say a woman has "given her husband the best years of her life" or a missionary couple have given themselves to "tireless service" in a foreign country.

Pondering statements like these has led me to a question: *Just whom do we think these people are serving?* Ken has not given his life to serve a handicapped woman. He's given his life to serve Christ. He just happens to be married to someone with a disability.

It's the same with anyone who serves in the Lord's name. How can service to the Lord Christ be a tedious, boring effort—or even a sacrifice? Certainly we tire of our service to people, "causes," organizations, companies, or academic institutions. No doubt Ken gets very tired of helping me through my nightly routine. I get tired, too.

31

Yet, however tiring our work may be, how could it ever be *tiresome?* How could it be anything less than a joy to serve the One who has given us all things for life and enrichment and enjoyment—Jesus, who suffered so much to secure our salvation.

Have you ever sensed a lack of purpose in your work? Have you struggled to see the reward for all your effort? Is it all getting a little wearisome?

It's the motive that counts. Doing your work wholeheartedly "as for the Lord" and not for the notice and praise of others can transform virtually any task you're called on to perform…whether it's counting widgets in a widget factory, writing a term paper in economics, cleaning the kitchen for the umpteenth time, or giving loving care to someone who fails to acknowledge or appreciate you.

The Lord Jesus will neither overlook nor forget the tasks you perform in His name. Nor will He fail to reward you.

STRONGHOLD

Is there someone in your family you've been caring for? Do you perform your tasks to impress others or to serve and praise God? This week read the book of Ruth and learn from it the principles of higher service.

SHADOWS

*The shadow of a mighty Rock within a
weary land...*

One of my favorite times of the day is late afternoon when shadows steal across our backyard. Ken and I like to pour a cool drink and sit out back, quietly watching the shadows shift and change. We position our chairs in the shade of our neighbor's big pine to escape the heat of the California sun. Trouble is, we have to keep inching our chairs to the left to keep up with that shadow.

Shadows. Always moving, changing with the seasons, shifting with the sun, never constant, never the same. The comfort we seek from them is temporary at best. Like Jonah crouching under the gourd vine, we find shadows fickle friends.

Ah, but there is Someone who casts an unchanging shadow. James 1:17 tells us that, "Every good thing bestowed and every perfect gift is from above, coming down from the Father of lights, with whom there is no variation, or shifting shadow."

That shadow never shifts, because our Father never changes. He's not evolving, as some theologians would have us believe. He's not transmutable, as other religions profess. No, He is constant and changeless. Always compassionate. Always merciful. Always just. Always holy. Always full of love.

The relief we find in His presence does not change with the passing of the hours, days, or years. The encouragement we find in His promises will not fail us when the heat of adversity bears down upon us. The security we find in His character will never vary though our lives turn upside down and the world changes around us.

How wonderful to have His shadow fall across us. Psalm 91 begins by saying, "He who dwells in the shelter of the Most High will abide in the shadow of the Almighty." The psalmist goes on to detail the many ways God protects His own, making them feel secure. In verses 11-12 we're told, "For He will give His angels charge concerning you, to guard you in all your ways. They will bear you up in their hands, lest you strike your foot against a stone."

Psalm 121 assures us that: "The LORD watches over you—the LORD is your shade at your right hand; the sun will not harm you by day, nor the moon by night. The LORD will keep you from all harm—he will watch over your life" (vv. 5-7, NIV).

You may fail Him, but He will never fail you. Place your chair in the shadow of the cross, and you will never have to move it.

STRONGHOLD

Read Isaiah 25:4-5. Describe the relief you have felt sitting in the shade on a hot summer day, thinking of at least three ways you were comforted. Have you felt the same kind of comfort resting in the shadow of God's presence?

STRENGTH...WHILE YOU WAIT

They will mount up with wings like eagles.

ISAIAH 40:31

Years ago my family and I took a camping trip up into the wilderness reserve of Jasper Provincial Park in Alberta, Canada. I remember boarding a chairlift that cabled us to the top of a huge, glacier-scarred mountain overlooking a broad expanse of pine forest below. There I marveled at the sight of a soaring eagle moving far across the wooded valley—just a tiny speck against the distant mountain range. I watched as the eagle circled and dove, admiring his grace and ease.

Eagles seem to go with big things—mountains, canyons, great depths, immense heights. It's always at the most stupendous and alluring spectacles of nature that we find them.

God talks about eagles. In one of the best-loved passages of the Old Testament, Isaiah 40:30-31, He uses their flight to describe the adventure that will unfold to the suffering Christian who waits for Him.

Most of us think of "waiting" as passive, something we have to do before the "real action" begins, a wearisome means to a better end. We wait in line at a grocery checkout counter, watch the clock on the wall at the dentist's office, glance at our watch while in a bank teller's line.

But waiting on God is far different. It's not passive, it's active. And it's not as though we *first* wait and *then* finally get the chance to mount up with wings, run without tiring, and walk without weariness. No, those good things actually happen *while* we are waiting! Waiting on God is an active, confident trusting...an instant obedience.

Isaiah promises a new and exciting perspective when we wait on the Lord. Waiting on God gives us the kind of perspective that an eagle must have. Our surroundings come into focus. Our horizons are broadened. We see our place in the scheme of things.

Waiting on God means confidently trusting that God knows how much I need and can take. It means looking expectantly toward the time when He will free me from my burdens. God's promise is clear. Those who wait for Him in their distress will receive strength and endurance which others know nothing about.

My body is now held by the limits of this wheelchair. But the waiting hope I have in God's future for me gives me the freedom to soar to heights of joy and explore the canyon depths of God's tender mercies.

All in all, it's worth the wait.

STRONGHOLD

How would you describe the difference between "passive" and "active" waiting? Read Hosea 12:6 and Psalm 25:4-7. What do these verses advise us to do while we wait?

GOD CHOOSES THE WEAK

*My grace is sufficient for you, for my
power is made perfect in weakness.*

2 CORINTHIANS 12:9, NIV

Have you ever thought of the Bible as an adventure story?

The King's most trusted officer turns renegade, gathers a powerful army around him, and leads a rebellion. Through treachery and deceit, the rebel leader usurps the authority of the rightful King, sets up his own rival government, and enslaves the citizens of the Kingdom. In order to free the captives and retake the Kingdom, the King sends His own Son into the heart of enemy territory...with a battle plan more shocking than anyone could imagine.

It sounds like epic fiction or the plot for an action adventure movie. But it's not. The battle blazes white-hot even as you read these words. Ceaseless warfare is being waged for the hearts and minds of men and women, boys and girls. The stakes are high, the consequences eternal.

Now, if I were God, seeking to gather a winning team around Jesus Christ, how would I get the job done?

Well, I'd need a strong economic base. So I'd go after the best brain trust I could pull together—all the Wall Street wizards, Harvard economists, and Fortune 500 guys. For my strategy team, I'd go after Nobel Prize laureates, MIT computer analysts, and the brightest men and women from the professional world. Umm...for public relations I'd hire some big Madison Avenue firm and a front man, of course...probably a rugged looking actor with a deep voice and a recognizable face. And maybe the president's chief of staff for a tough-minded manager.

But *I'm* not running the world, God is. And He has already written the most magnificent script imaginable for invading Satan's territory and retaking the Kingdom of Earth under the banner of His Son. But He has peopled the script with the weak and the poor and the unlikely. He casts the roles employing the sick, the lonely, the ungifted, and the unlovely as Paul says so well in in his first letter to the Corinthians.

He's chosen such people on His team for a special reason. You see, Satan scoffs at the insignificant, average, everyday sort of folks the Lord crowds onto His team. But this is the catch. If God, by sheer grace, overcomes in spite of the odds, winning the world by using weak and inferior people, guess Who receives even greater glory?

Now that's a story worth telling.

STRONGHOLD

If you were to lead an army against a host of hostile foreigners, how many people would you want? For a good story on how God delights to use weak people (and weakened armies!) read Judges chapter 7.

THOUGHTS IN THE CORNER

He who did not spare his own Son,…will
he not…graciously give us all things?

ROMANS 8:32, NIV

here you are. In the corner again. Facing an ago-
nizing choice—a do-or-die challenge. Yes, God
is asking you to come through for Him once
again.

Do I hear a murmur in your heart of hearts? A faint
note of protest? *Now, come on, God, what do You expect
from me? Blood? None of my friends seems to be faced with
such faith-challenging, heart-wrenching tests. What do you
think I am? Some kind of martyr?*

Back in the corner. We've all stood where you're standing, at one time or another. We've all toyed with the
thought that, just maybe, God might be asking too much
of us.

To set the record straight, what does the Bible say
about all this? The writer of Deuteronomy has an
answer—and what an answer it is! "What does the LORD
your God ask of you but to fear the LORD your God, to
walk in all his ways, to love him, to serve the LORD your
God with all your heart and with all your soul, and to
observe the LORD's commands and decrees that I am giving you today for your own good?" (Deuteronomy 10:12-
13, NIV).

What does God ask of us? Only to fear Him…to love
Him…to serve Him…to obey Him—*and to do so with*

all our heart and with all our soul.

All God is asking for is everything.

Early on in my disability there were times when I felt He was asking too much of me. I felt like a martyr. That martyr complex, I've come to realize, was fostered by concentrating too much on what God asked of me—and not enough on what God had *given* me.

If you're tempted to think that "everything" sounds like too much, stop a moment and consider what God has given you. How much did *He* hold back? Anything? Of course not. In fact, He gave more than everything. He gave His own life, His own Son.

That's the beauty behind it all, isn't it? For if we're tempted to get a little fainthearted, let's remember that God has promised us even more than His own Son. He's promised us power through the Spirit—power that will help us do all that He asks of us...power that will strengthen our weak knees and faint hearts. As Paul put it, "I can do all things through Him who strengthens me" (Philippians 4:13).

So what does God expect of you today? Does it seem like a bit too much? Do you feel backed into a corner? Remember, all He asks from you is everything. And all He offers you is the power to do just that.

STRONGHOLD

When you look at today's responsibilities, do you feel God expects too much of you? If so, read Romans 8:31-32 and Ephesians 3:14-21 for strength and encouragement.

THE REFUGE

The Lord is my rock and my fortress.
PSALM 18:2

I treasure happy memories of my sister Kathy and me constructing a special tree house when we lived on the farm. It was some distance from the farmhouse, so it was private—far away from the intruding eyes of grownups. We lugged wood and confiscated nails and borrowed hammers and put together a very fine and well-constructed house (or at least we thought so) up in the inviting arms of an old tree.

A shelter? A place to hide? Oh yes, but it was more than that to me. In my childish thinking it was a *fortress*— a high tower soaring above the wild frontiers! The storms would swirl and howl outside of that little house, the rain would beat on the tin roof, and the wind would make the house sway in the branches of the tree. But we were safe. Protected. Dry and cozy.

Don't you ever find yourself wishing it were that easy again? Because the storms don't stop as we grow up, do they? The clouds can become darker than we ever imagined, and the wind can shake us with a fury that seems more than we can endure. Sometimes, we long for a hiding place.

We're not alone in that desire. Even some of the greatest men in the Bible expressed such a longing. In one of his deepest moments of pain and sorrow over the sin of his people, Jeremiah cried out to God (Jeremiah 9:1-6). There were times when David, too, wished with all his heart for a shelter from the storms of life, as in Psalm 55:6-8.

The wonderful thing about the Bible is that it doesn't leave us in our despair. Scripture tells us there is a hiding place. A shelter much stronger than a fragile refuge of our own making. Mightier than earth's most powerful citadel.

"The Lord is my rock and my fortress and my deliverer," wrote David, "My God, my rock, in whom I take refuge. My shield and the horn of my salvation, my stronghold...my God, in whom I trust! Under His wings you may seek refuge; His faithfulness is a shield and bulwark.... The Lord is with me; I will not be afraid. What can man do to me?" (Psalms 18:2; 91:2, 4; 118:6, NAS, NIV).

What better hiding place could there be? What better shelter for anxious hearts and weary minds? Climb up with me into His love, under His sheltering grace, and together, let's say, "The Lord is with us; we will not fear."

STRONGHOLD

Take a look at Hebrews 13:4-6. How does the Lord's beautiful offer of refuge, help, and security apply to these areas of our lives—sex and marriage and money?

v.4
"God w/ judge the adulterer and all the sexually immoral"

PRUNING

We too may live a new life.
ROMANS 6:4, NIV

t never fails. Each spring I'm amazed by those first, tentative signs…little green shoots poking out of the soil…little green buds bursting off the vine.

I'm amazed because I'm so *ruthless* with my clippers in the fall. I prune my plants and shrubbery unmercifully. Blossoms are severed as soon as they fade. Sturdy young branches are consigned to the dumpster. Nothing escapes the bite of those shears. Through the winter the Tada foliage looks stark, chastened, even lifeless.

But spring always changes things. As I pen these words on this first day of spring, life is beginning all over again in my garden.

So it's been since the beginning. Back in ancient Uz, the thoughts of a godly man named Job turned to spring—a spring he believed he would never see (see Job 14:7-12).

Job could not imagine a future renewal in his own life. The Lord's sharp shears had clipped his life so close to the roots he didn't see how it could ever grow back. Everything dear to him had been slashed away in cruel, successive strokes. "Only a few years will pass before I go on the journey of no return," he told his friends. "My spirit is broken, my days are cut short..." (16:22—17:1, NIV).

Like Job, at times we feel there's more hope for a fallen tree than for us. Like Job, we voice our questions and wrestle with our pain. God's pruning shears seem merciless. Nothing escapes the cutting edge of His will. Not the blossom of youth, not the bloom of good health, not the fruit of prosperity, not the sturdy, growing family.

But spring comes, doesn't it? Hope returns. New life pokes up from the dead stump. Joy reappears...ever so slowly, almost shyly, and not all at once. But it comes. Fresh new grace enables us to endure. Bright, hopeful promises offer a strong trellis to which we can cling. The sweet, heady fragrance of the Holy Spirit blows across our lives, waters us with His Word, and encourages us to reach for all the good things God has in store for us. Much to Job's amazement, spring even came to him (see Job 42:10-16).

In God's order, winter always gives way to spring. The iron grip of January yields to the sunshine of His love. If not now, then soon.

Spring will not tarry. New life is on the way.

STRONGHOLD

If you're going through a winter time in your soul, read Romans 6 today. To gain extra insight, read it once in your regular Bible and again in a paraphrase such as The Living Bible. *Let the promise of "newness of life" in verse 4 remind you that spring can begin today in your heart.*

A TOOL IN THE MASTER'S HAND

*The members of the body which seem
to be weaker are necessary.*

1 CORINTHIANS 12:22

J ames Sewell has been my art coach for many years now and has taught me wonderful things about the world of painting. Once Jim brought some of his own brushes from his studio. I was startled by the condition they were in. These brushes, he told me, were over thirty years old. Frankly, they looked it. The paint on the handles was worn and chipped. The brushes themselves were discolored and bristly and had obviously seen incredible wear.

If I hadn't known better, I would have said they were useless…not fit for painting anything of real beauty or value. But then I had the chance to watch Jim at work in front of his easel with those very brushes. Suddenly, in his hands, they became not only useful, but *priceless*. I marveled how each brush—even the ugliest one—had its own purpose. One brush for a certain kind of line, another for a special kind of stroke.

It was no surprise that he never even picked up one of my nice, new, soft sable brushes. No, he preferred to work with his well-worn, well-proven tools.

Someone once said that a tool unto itself is of little importance. But placed in the proper hands it can create a masterpiece.

That day as I watched Jim at work with his old brushes,

he created a beautiful painting right before my eyes. If I had placed those same brushes in my mouth, there's no way I could have created such a masterpiece. I'm simply not a master. But Jim had proven to me that any tool in his hand—even the most unlovely and unlikely—could be used with mighty purpose.

In a similar way, perhaps, you may find yourself thinking you're unfit for service in the kingdom of God. Your potential, you tell yourself, is small—maybe non-existent. You may feel you've gone through too much, wandered too far, or seen too much wear to accomplish anything wonderful for the Lord.

Ah, that's the problem with concentrating on the *tool.* Remember, no tool, in and of itself, has great importance. But placed in the proper hands it can create a masterpiece.

What an encouragement to realize that God has reserved you and me for a special task in His great work. In His hands we're not only useful…but priceless.

STRONGHOLD

Do you use a favorite old comb with missing teeth? Or a spatula that's been flipping pancakes for twenty years? In your hands, these trusted items perform best. Let these simple, everyday items remind you of how God has chosen you with your strengths and weaknesses for special tasks.

RESOURCES FOR THE JOURNEY

Lo, I am with you always.
MATTHEW 28:20

In her book *A Slow and Certain Light*, Elisabeth Elliot tells of two young adventurers who came to see her in Ecuador. The two men were on their way to the rain forests east of the Andes. Both were weighted down with huge packs of equipment—most of it more cumbersome than helpful. Yet they didn't want her evaluation of their supplies. Nor did they ask for counsel or advice about their trip. All they wanted were a few phrases of the Indian language. They were certain this was all they lacked to be fully prepared for their journey. She writes:

> Sometimes we come to God as the two adventurers came to me—confident and, we think, well-informed and well-equipped. But it has occurred to us that with all our accumulation of stuff something is missing. There is just one thing we will have to ask God for and we hope He will not find it necessary to sort through the other things. There's nothing there that we're willing to do without. We know what we need—a yes or no answer, please, to a simple question. Or perhaps a road sign. Something quick and easy to point the way.

What we really ought to have is the Guide Himself.

Maps, road signs, and a few useful phrases are good things, but infinitely better is Someone who has been there before and knows the way.[1]

You and I want all the maps, guides, and compasses we can get our hands on as we plan our journey into marriage, a career, or a family. We want the blueprint spread out before us if we're going through a crisis. We need to make sense out of our suffering. But through it all, Jesus says that He is with us always. It is His presence that makes the real difference between acceptance or anger, hope or despair.

Jesus Christ has been there ahead of us. He knows the way. He understands the journey and, what's more, He offers to walk with us through it all.

Maps and guidebooks are fine. But when the sky grows dark and the path gets rough, our best resource is the Guide Himself.

STRONGHOLD

Have you ever asked a person for directions and left more confused than ever? Have you wished that person would say, "Follow me. I'm headed that direction"? Jesus said virtually the same thing in John 14:5-6. Thank your Lord right now that He does not hand you an impossible creed as a road map for life. He offers you Himself!

1. Elisabeth, Elliott, *A Slow and Certain Light* (Nashville, Tenn.: Abingdon Press, 1982).

RELYING ON GOD

The rock of my strength, my refuge is in God.

PSALM 62:7

While having lunch with a quadriplegic friend the other day, I started talking about the help and encouragement I've received from my relationship with Christ.

My friend, however, wasn't happy at all about that turn in our conversation. "Jesus can't help me," he frowned. "It isn't Jesus who helps me with this sandwich; it's my friend here," he said, motioning to the person sitting next to him who was cutting up his food. "And Jesus doesn't put me to bed at night or get me up in the morning or get me a drink of water. It's *people* I need."

What a shortsighted view this man had of our God. All he could think of was the immediate and urgent needs of his paralysis. He couldn't look past his handicap.

The apostle Paul has advice for people who get shortsighted about their suffering. Bruised and battered, he writes in 2 Corinthians that he was under great pressure, far beyond his ability to endure. Reflecting on those horrendous circumstances, the apostle makes this statement: "But this happened that we might not rely on ourselves but on God" (1:9, NIV).

Few of us will ever face the sorts of hardships Paul encountered, but his assurance can still be ours. You and I can look at the disappointments which wound and bewilder us and say with resolve that these things have happened that we might not rely on ourselves, but on God.

Being a quadriplegic means I have no use of my hands or legs. Like my friend, I need someone else to floss my teeth or hold a cup to my lips so I can drink. Somebody has to tuck in my blouse when it pulls out of my slacks. If I get too hot, someone has to reach for the ice or the fan. Someone has to help me in and out of bed. There's hardly an hour of the day that I don't rely on the willing hands and feet of others.

But I've learned not to be so shortsighted about my disability and the people who help me. It is Jesus who feeds me my sandwich. After all, He's the one who provides that friend sitting next to me, just as He provides the food. It is Jesus who lovingly works through my husband when he helps me in bed at night. And it is Jesus who brings people to help me in the morning.

If I ever ask you to help me with a sandwich or hold a coffee cup for me, I'll smile my thanks at you…but give Him the glory.

STRONGHOLD

We often depend on our own skills and abilities when life seems easy, turning to God only when we've exhausted other resources. Dependence is not defeat; it is glorious. Read what David, a powerful warrior and king, wrote on the subject in Psalm 62, especially verses 7-8.

LIFELINE

The LORD is good to those who wait for him.
LAMENTATIONS 3:25, NKJV

Those early days when I first got out of the hospital were terrifying. Without the encouragement and perspective of Scripture, I honestly don't know how I would have survived. Like a strong lifeline, God's Word kept me from drowning in my despair. Several of those "lifeline" passages were from a single chapter in the book of Lamentations—chapter 3.

In verse 25, Jeremiah wrote that the Lord is good to those who wait for Him. What else did I have to do but wait? The long, lonely hours in the middle of the night were bearable because of that promise. God would be good. To me. I was waiting, and knew I would see His goodness.

In verse 26 the prophet goes on to say that one should hope and wait for salvation. Salvation, deliverance. It was a promise, right there in black and white. I clung to that hope with all that was in me. I waited and believed that deliverance (whatever that meant) would surely come.

In the very next verse, Jeremiah says, "It is good for a man to bear the yoke in his youth" (3:27, NKJV). Some things are harder to learn as we get older. Our hearts may be calloused or indifferent. Perhaps age brings the feeling of being worldly wise—we've "seen it all," and there is nothing new to learn. For all the pain of shattered dreams, a yoke is better borne in youth.

As a young teenager, my heart was still tender. I was still hammering out values and principles. So I gritted my teeth and trusted that it was good to bear such a heavy yoke of disability in my youth.

But the best part of Lamentations 3 was in verses 31-32: "For the Lord will not cast off forever. Though He causes grief, yet He will show compassion according to the multitude of His mercies" (NKJV). That verse was like a light at the end of the tunnel for me. To know that things wouldn't be like this forever! Though God had His hand in my injury, He would also show compassion. He had helped me through the long nights. He would be with me during the lonely days of adjusting to my wheelchair.

The yoke? Yes, it's still heavy to bear. But time and again God in His grace has thrown out the sturdy lifeline of His Word just when I felt I was about to go under.

Look…there's a lifeline in front of you, too. Grab on like never before. He'll never let you sink.

STRONGHOLD

Jeremiah wrote Lamentations, the "book of lamenting," during the crisis of the Babylonian invasion. Look at 3:22-24. How about verse 33 for encouragement? And verse 40 is a real lifesaver. Facing tough times today? Grab hold of these lifeline verses.

3:22,23 The Lord's love never ends; His mercies never stop, They are new every morning; Lord your loyalty is great.

A MATTER OF THE HEART

Now we have received, not the spirit of the world, but the Spirit who is from God.

1 CORINTHIANS 2:12

O ur church has a class for mentally handicapped children and young people. It's a happy group where the students enjoy learning to pray and hearing stories about Jesus, illustrated by puppets and flannelgraphs.

One young girl in the class has been grasping the ideas quickly, thirstily absorbing spiritual content. Her mother recently called the church elder for special ministries to express her amazement. "I don't understand it," she said. "My daughter is picking up things I *know* she can't understand. Yet she's learning—far beyond her natural capabilities."

The woman can't believe her eyes and ears. But none of this takes our elder by surprise. For him this is just one more example of the truth in 1 Corinthians 2 about the teachings by the Spirit. Time after time he's seen God's Spirit teach mentally handicapped persons truths far beyond their natural capabilities to comprehend.

We tend to think the brighter you are the more of God's Word you'll understand. Not so, this scripture teaches us. The message of Jesus Christ crucified is not imparted through plausible words of human wisdom, but "in demonstration of the Spirit and of power, that your faith should not rest on the wisdom of men, but on the power of God" (1 Corinthians 2:4-5).

Remember the story of Peter's confession? Late in His ministry, Jesus turned to His disciples with a penetrating question: "Who do you say that I am?"

"You are the Christ," Simon Peter answered, "the Son of the living God."

Jesus replied, "Blessed are you, Simon son of Jonah, *for this was not revealed to you by man, but by my Father in heaven"* (see Matthew 16:13-17, NIV).

It's interesting that Jesus did not commend Peter for his brainpower. Peter's answer had nothing to do with acute observation, logical perception, intellectual prowess, or formal theological training.

You don't need a seminary degree and an elevated IQ to discern spiritual truth. According to 1 Corinthians 2:16, we have the mind of Christ. Yes, even a mentally handicapped child has the mind of Jesus!

Walking with God isn't a matter of the intellect, it's a matter of the heart.

STRONGHOLD

When it comes to discerning spiritual truth, we are all mentally handicapped apart from the teaching and guidance of the Spirit of God. With this in mind, read John 14:16-17, 25-27. Exactly what will the Spirit teach you? Take a few moments and thank God for His Holy Spirit's working through, for, and with you.

OPEN MY EYES

So the LORD opened their eyes, and they saw.
2 KINGS 6:20

Bent on destroying the prophet Elisha, the king of Syria received reliable information that the man he sought was living in the walled city of Dothan. The king wasn't taking any chances. Rather than sending a couple of hit men to liquidate Elisha, the king mobilized "horses and chariots and a great army" (2 Kings 6:14). The massive Syrian force came by night and surrounded the city, readying for an early-morning assault.

At daybreak, Elisha's servant went out for a casual stroll along the top of the wall. What he saw must have made the blood freeze in his veins. The morning sun gleamed and flashed from countless shields, helmets, chariot wheels, arrows, and spear tips. Filled with sheer terror, the attendant scampered back to the prophet's chamber with the tidings of gloom and doom. His servant said, "Alas, my master! What shall we do?" (6:15).

If the servant was expecting his master to fly into a panic or tear out what remained of his sparse hair, he was in for a surprise. He was probably even more surprised by Elisha's calm reply: "Do not fear, for those who are with us are more than those who are with them" (6:16). Elisha was not afraid of the Syrian king and his intimidating army. For he trusted in One who could not be seen with the physical eye.

But Elisha did more than give a devotional homily to his frightened servant. He prayed for him, saying, "O LORD, I pray, open his eyes that he may see." The Lord answered and the servant saw..."and behold, the mountain was full of horses and chariots of fire all around Elisha" (6:17).

I like that story. Because when we're serving the Lord, fighting off temptation, or making a stand against fear, we may feel lonely on our side of the battle lines. The devil has his troops marshaled against us! Bastions of secularism. Strong political lobbies. Pornography running rampant. Racism. Injustice. Stumbling Christian leaders.

At such a time when fear grips your heart and your faith weakens and wavers, pray that the Lord will open your eyes...that you may see. There's no less of a force surrounding you on the front lines of the battlefield as there was in Elisha's day. A host of angels? A legion of saints? A mountain of horses and chariots of fire? Probably. But all you really need is the One who promised never to leave or forsake you—the One who said, "Lo, I am with you always."

STRONGHOLD

Do you feel overwhelmed by the forces that seem arrayed against you? Read Ephesians 1:15-23. What sorts of things should you be able to see when God gives you the "eyes of the heart" described in verse 18?

"SURPRISING" TRIALS

Rejoice in the Lord always.
PHILIPPIANS 4:4

I just can't get used to trials. Every time I get hit broadside with a fresh dose of trouble, my first response is, *Whoa! Where in the world did that come from? God picked me to handle this?*

Like the other day when my van had a flat tire. My first thought was, *God, you've got the wrong person for this one. Remember? This is Joni—the one who's paralyzed. I can't exactly hop out, flip open the trunk, grab the jack and spin on a spare! Good grief, I can't even flag down a passer-by or thumb a ride to a local gas station.*

Frankly, I was surprised. But guess what verse kept floating its way to the top of my thinking? "Dear friends, do not be surprised at the painful trial you are suffering, as though something strange were happening to you" (1 Peter 4:12, NIV).

For as many times as I've fallen into trials, they still come as a surprise. It seems I would have learned that lesson from reading that verse in Peter so many times.

But James, Peter's cohort, has some sage advice for people like me. "Consider it all joy, my brethren, when you encounter various trials," he writes, "knowing that the testing of your faith produces endurance" (James 1:2-3).

Could James actually be expecting us to paste on a plastic smile when we fall headlong into heartaches? Not at all. James says, *"Consider it all joy."* In other words, reckon or regard it; make a conscious acceptance of the fact. The response he is speaking of has more to do with our minds than our emotions.

Why should we regard our problems with joy? Because we *know* something, says James. We know that those trials are producing endurance in our lives—patience, maturity, and all-around good character.

Today—right now—I want to resolve to know something about the intruder that will invariably knock on my door. Before I get up to answer his knock, I want to remember that this unwelcome visitor, for all his ill manners, has come for *my good*, for the good of my character. No matter what my emotions tell me, I want to welcome him in. Why? Because down deep, real character is more important to me than temporary comfort.

Will you resolve the same thing with me today? Let's greet that surprise intruder with a surprise of our own.

Joy.

STRONGHOLD

Paul was a good one for greeting trials with a joyful mind-set. Just take a look at Philippians 2:12-18; 4:4-7. Even though Paul was writing from prison, his letter is full of joy. In fact, the words joy *or* rejoice *are used fourteen times in Philippians. Take time to memorize Philippians 4:4 and make it your "verse of welcome" when your next trial sneaks up on you.*

GOD'S GOODNESS: OUR RESPONSE

*Do you show contempt for the riches of his kindness,
tolerance and patience, not realizing that God's kindness
leads you toward repentance?*

ROMANS 2:4, NIV

L ast Easter, like most of you, I read through the
story of the crucifixion to prepare my heart for
Easter morning. And I found myself deliberating over the words of Christ when He cried in anguish
from the cross, "My God, my God, why have you forsaken
me?"

I have to admit it. The idea that the Father would
allow His Son to suffer the torture of crucifixion is
beyond me. The humiliation of nakedness, the searing
pain, the smell of blood and sweat, the agony of tears, the
spit of drunken soldiers, the scorn of a jeering mob. As
tears mingled with blood on His battered face, Jesus cried
out to His Father—the One who had not once turned
away from Him in all of eternity.

The reply was silence. Cold, accusing silence.

Heaven itself accused Jesus of sins in those horrible
moments: lusting and lying, cheating and coveting, murder and hypocrisy, cruelty and deceit. Of course, Christ
had never been guilty of any of those sins, *but we are*. And
every one of your sins and mine was racked up on His
account right there on that cross, as the prophet Isaiah testified in Isaiah 53:4-6 and as Paul wrote in Colossians
2:13-15.

So where was God's goodness in treating Christ so? Where was the Father's kindness in turning His back on His only Son—while Jesus cried out in horror and grief?

On that terrible, wonderful day, God's goodness and kindness were directed toward you. God forsook His own Son...so that He would never have to forsake you! And because of those dark hours two thousand years ago, God can say to me, "I will never leave you, Joni. I will never forsake you."

As I pondered that amazing thought, I felt ashamed. The goodness of God was leading me to repentance. To think that God's anger for my sins was poured out on Christ—and that He has no anger left for me!

You know what that makes me want to do? Praise Him. Thank Him. Honor Him. Obey Him with all my heart and soul and mind. Unlike Christ, I will _never_ have to agonize over separation from my Father. And neither will you. God poured the full measure of His wrath—the terrors of eternal hell—on His own Son...so that you and I could be adopted into His very family. That's how much He loves you. And me.

STRONGHOLD

Flip to the end of Matthew's gospel and marvel at the last three verses. Jesus went through heaven and hell to assure you with this last, great statement He made on earth. Let His goodness right now crumble any resistance in your heart and lead you into a prayer of repentance.

28:20 "I will be with you always..."

WHO HELPS THE MOST?

The greatest of these is love.
1 CORINTHIANS 13:13

People will often ask me, "Who helped you the most when you were hurting?"

That's a good question, but I can never seem to come up with a fast answer. I guess that's because there was no one person—no famous writer, no brainy seminary student, no super-sensitive counselor.

No, answers to my questions didn't come from "extraordinary" people. Frankly, when I was first injured in my diving accident and left paralyzed, I wasn't *looking* for wisdom or knowledge.

At first I was just looking for love.

That should be good news to those of you looking for ways to alleviate the pain of a friend in the hospital or a family member going through a crushing disappointment. If you and I are truly looking for an answer to the question, "How do I help those who are in pain?" we don't have to have a lot of answers. We don't even have to know all the specialized scriptures or a hundred and one reasons why God allows suffering. All we've got to know is love. The only scripture we might need at first is 1 Corinthians 13.

I most appreciated those people who came into the hospital armed with love—and *Seventeen* magazines and Winchell's doughnuts. I appreciated friends dropping by to help me write letters or to bring me writing paper and envelopes—even stamps. I was super-impressed when others bought birthday cards for me to send to a friend whose special day was coming up. I especially remember a few girls who made it a weekly ritual to come by and do my nails. What fun!

These were people who helped. They weren't trained counselors. They weren't spiritual giants. They weren't biblical wizards. They weren't Ph.D.'s. They weren't even full of all kinds of knowledge and wisdom. They were just commonplace, everyday sorts of people who gave me what I needed most of all…God's love in action.

STRONGHOLD

Love, as it says in the last verse of 1 Corinthians 12, is "the most excellent way" to reach out to someone who's hurting. Why not take this chance to read 1 Corinthians 13 and think of ways you can exhibit these traits of love with a hurting friend who needs His supernatural love.

WHEN GOD OPENS THE SHUTTERS

And I saw a new heaven and a new earth.

REVELATION 21:1

I f our happiest moments on earth give us a fore-taste of heaven, then the tragic moments make us long for it.

The truth of the matter is I never used to think much about heaven when I was on my feet. It seemed like some vague, distant, misty place where there would be a lot of clouds and harps and we'd polish gold all day—forever! That prospect seemed very unattractive to me—and immensely boring.

Besides, in order to get to heaven, you had to *die*. And at the age of seventeen who wants to think about that?

But heaven is so wonderful, it's just like God to give us a little help to turn our thoughts toward that future reality. And sometimes it takes more than a lovely starlit night or a verse of Scripture to open our eyes.

Samuel Rutherford describes this help in an essay he wrote back in the seventeenth century: "If God had told me some time ago that He was about to make me as happy as I could be in this world and then had told me that He should begin by crippling me in arm or limb and removing from me all my usual sources of enjoyment, I should have thought it a very strange mode of accomplishing His purpose. And yet, how is His wisdom manifest even in this. For if you should see a man shut up in a closed room idolizing a set of lamps and rejoicing in their light and you wished to make him truly happy, you would begin by blowing out all of his lamps and then throw open the shutters to let in the light of heaven."[2]

That's just what God did for me when He sent a broken neck my way. He blew out all the lamps in my life which lit up the here and now and made it so exciting. To be sure, the dark depression that followed wasn't much fun. But it certainly made the prospect of heaven come to life. My heart leaps to think of the day when I'll have my new body—hands that feel, arms that hold, and legs that run.

One day God will throw open the shutters. The view that fills our eyes in that moment will make us forget all about the lamps in our shuttered room.

Do you find yourself all caught up in the here and now? Do you sometimes feel a slave to the clock? Are you sick and tired of struggling with sin or the anxieties and sorrows that weigh down your heart? God may be using those very things to turn your thoughts toward your future home...and the One who awaits the sound of your steps at the front door.

STRONGHOLD

Read Revelation 21 to help you throw open the shutters of heaven today. Consider verse 21. What things will hold value in heaven? How can you lay up the kind of treasure which will last for eternity?

2. Samuel Rutherford (1600-1661), the Letters of Samuel Rutherford (Banner of Truth, 1985 reprint).

HANDHOLDS IN HIS CHARACTER

*He who began a good work in you will carry it
on to completion.*

PHILIPPIANS 1:6

hen I was emerging from my depression over being paralyzed, I uncovered a promise in the Bible about God's faithfulness. Philippians 1:6 told me to be *confident,* in fact, of this one thing: that He who had begun a good work in me would carry it on to completion until the day of Christ Jesus.

You have to put that promise within the context of my life at that time. For the first time since the accident, I was trying to peer into my future. Yet it seemed as though a thick, black curtain hung just inches in front of my face. The appalling reality of a *lifetime* of paralysis was almost more than I could bear. My faith seemed paralyzed, too. It was hard to imagine how anything good would come out of it. I was convinced I would never smile again.

But when I came across Philippians 1:6, immediately I grabbed hold of the faithfulness of God. I took hold of His tenderness and His mercy. I quoted the verse to the Lord asking Him to fulfill His promise of completing a good—yes, a *very good*—work in my life.

And do you know what? I found peace. I was confident that God, in His faithfulness, would hold Himself to His promise.

Charles Spurgeon once said, "You and I may take hold at anytime upon the justice, mercy, faithfulness, wisdom, longsuffering, [or] tenderness of God, and we shall find every attribute of the Most High to be, as it were, a great battering ram with which we may open the gates of heaven."

Abraham, pleading with God to spare Sodom, reminded the Lord, "Shall not the Judge of all the earth do right?" (Genesis 18:25, NKJV). Did God need a reminder? "Oh, thanks, Abe. I'd completely forgotten that angle. Thanks for jogging My memory." Obviously, God did not need a nudge to remember His justice. Yet He was delighted that Abraham sought heavenly justice on the merits of the heavenly Judge. Abraham pleaded his case from the platform of God's character.

How about you? Do you involve God in your prayer? Do you find handholds and footholds in His character? Do you plead with Him on the basis of Who He is? Consider again His justice, His mercy, His faithfulness, His wisdom, His purity, His might, and His tenderness. Humbly hold Him to His promises. God is delighted when you seek His will, His character, His glory—and yes, His heart—in your prayers.

STRONGHOLD

Pick an attribute of God and meditate for a few moments on how marvelously God reveals Himself through that attribute. Then in your prayers during the rest of the day link all of your requests to that special attribute of your heavenly Father.

THE PROCESS IS THE END

LORD,...let me know how transient I am.

PSALM 39:4

Tens of thousands of students are sweating their way through midterm exams as I write these words. They're thinking about declaring their major or deciding on postgraduate work or wondering where marriage fits in—if at all.

Their minds are on the future. It seems everything they do right now has an incredible bearing on where they will be next year. Today's domino is going to fall squarely on tomorrow's.

You and I tend to feel the same way, don't we? We feel that we're in training for "something in the future." And every decision we make is a link in a long chain of events that will culminate in some final, better situation. Then and only then will we have "arrived." But in the meantime, we've got to do double duty to make certain we're in the middle of God's will. Don't want to take a wrong turn. Don't want to make a second-best decision.

God, we assure ourselves, is leading us to a particular end, a desired goal. But sometimes the question of *getting* there is merely incidental.

You see, what we call "the process"—the process of getting there—God calls "the end." God's training is for *right now,* not for some mist-shrouded future. His purpose is for this minute, not for something better down the road.

67

His power and His presence are available to you as you draw your next breath, not for some great impending struggle.

This moment is the future for which you've been preparing!

James, the Lord's brother, brings us up short in our preoccupation with tomorrow (James 4:13-16). In God's economy, it is *today* that is of utmost importance. The way you cling to Christ today, the opportunities you maximize today, the conversations you engage in, or the acts of kindness you perform today are the most critical activities of your entire life. And who this side of heaven knows how God may use them?

Oswald Chambers has said, "What you call preparation, God calls the end. And if you have a further end in view, then perhaps you are not paying sufficient attention to the immediate present."

STRONGHOLD

Do you occasionally find yourself grasping for the future as though the present didn't quite satisfy? Do you sometimes feel you miss the best of life while looking the other way, preoccupied with shaping your future? Look up Psalm 39:4 and make it your prayer today.

WORKMANSHIP

*For we are God's workmanship, created in Christ Jesus
to do good works.*

EPHESIANS 2:10, NIV

I t's so much fun to be a painter. One of my favorite times of day is when I wheel into the art studio, close the door behind me, and maneuver my chair in front of my easel. There, a whole world opens up to me.

As an artist, I can express my deepest thoughts and wishes on canvas. I can paint mountains which inspire and elevate the thinking of those who view the rendering. I can evoke calmness and peace with a gently rolling seascape. Through works of art, a painter can teach, uplift, and communicate all sorts of helpful and positive qualities.

Our great, creative God does the same thing in each of our lives. Paul says in Ephesians 2:10 that we are God's "workmanship." The Greek word translated "workmanship" here is *poiema*, which means a work of art or a specially designed product.

Do you see what Scripture is saying? Each one of us is God's special work of art. Through us, He teaches and inspires, delights and encourages, informs and uplifts all those who view our lives. God, the master artist, is most concerned about expressing Himself—His thoughts and His intentions—through what He paints in our character. Each unchangeable part, each weakness, each strength, is like a brush stroke in the complete composition He has in mind for us. Our master artist takes time to mix the colors He wants to portray through our character.

Maybe you don't feel much like a "work of art" today. I understand. If you saw the beginning stages of some of my paintings, you'd wonder if anything of beauty could *ever* emerge from such a confusion of colors. Just remember…the master artist wants to paint a beautiful portrait of His Son in and through your life. A painting like no other in all of time.

And He isn't finished yet.

STRONGHOLD

Just think! You are a work of art. Just as the potter will shape and mold a piece of clay into a beautiful vase, God touches your life with His creative genius. Read about it in Jeremiah 18:1-6, and rejoice that He has chosen the perfect design just for you!

COMFORTING LIGHT

He who practices the truth comes to the light.

JOHN 3:21

I was a child who was scared of the dark. I didn't like being the first one through the front door to flick on the lights. And things didn't change much even after I became a teenager. I'd come home from a date and dread to see the house dark. Turning the key in the front lock and creaking open the door, I'd call, "Anybody home?"

In the dark, shapes take on eerie silhouettes. True meanings are obscured. We're frightened by the unfamiliar.

But what a comfort light is! Light reveals things for what they really are.

As we read Scripture, we realize that it didn't take God very long to "turn on the light." In the second verse of the Bible, the author describes a brooding, primordial darkness. But in the very next verse, God says, "Let there be light."

As I pondered that statement recently, comparing it with other verses in Genesis 1, I discovered that God wasn't talking about the light of the sun, moon, or stars. God didn't form the light-bearing heavenly bodies until later, on creation's fourth day. So what could He mean? Where was the light coming from?

I checked a couple of cross references and noted this verse in John 1: "In the beginning was the Word, and the

Word was with God, and the Word was God" (v. 1).

Can you imagine the scene? God is ready to begin creation. The script is written, the play is about to commence. The curtain is closed, the stage is empty, and there's darkness all around. But God, much like the director of a great, moving drama, begins the play. "Let there be light," He shouts, and the central character of creation steps out to take the leading role. Jesus, the Light of the world, the Creator and Sustainer of creation, walks out on stage in the middle of His own spotlight.

What a thought! How thrilled I was to see Jesus, the Alpha and Omega, as described in the last book of the Bible, spotlighted in the very beginning of the first book of the Bible. Truly, God's Word begins and ends with Christ.

He who is the Light of creation now says, "You are the light of the world." He has given you and me the responsibility to reveal reality in a dark, sin-blinded world—to show things for what they really are.

People are afraid. People are confused, bewildered, and in despair. It's time to let the Light shine.

STRONGHOLD

Read John 3:16-21. Why do some people refuse to "see the Light"? Perhaps they're afraid the light may expose some darkness in their lives. Keep praying they will come to see how much better it is to live in light rather than darkness. In fact, why not pray for them right now?

LOVE IS EXTRAVAGANT

But the greatest of these is love.
1 CORINTHIANS 13:13

I had just finished packing my bags. Ken had packed his things, too, including his rods and reels. We had to be away from one another for several days—I on a speaking engagement, and he on a fishing trip. We knew we'd really miss each other.

Wheeling through the living room that afternoon, I was surprised to see a beautiful red rose in a bud vase on the table. That Ken! So thoughtful. Moving into the bedroom to gather my things, I spotted *another* rose in a bud vase on my dresser. I was shocked. I glanced in the bathroom and to my amazement yet *another* red rose—a fresh, delicate, little bud—adorned the counter.

By the third rose, I have to admit my excitement turned sour. It wasn't that I didn't appreciate his gifts, it was just that...well, both he and I were ready to leave. Nobody but our miniature schnauzer Scruffy would be in the house to enjoy such lovely flowers. *Expensive* flowers at that, I pointed out.

Ken gave me a big hug that melted my protests.

As I went off on that speaking trip, I thought of the quality that marks the ministry of love. And that is its sheer *extravagance*. Love is extravagant in the price it is willing to pay, the time it is willing to give, the hardships it is willing to endure, and the strength it is willing to spend.

Love never thinks in terms of "how little," but always in terms of "how much."

And that is what God has given to us. The quality that marks the ministry of God's love for us is the sheer extravagance of giving His most priceless and precious gift—His Son. When the Father considered ransoming sinful, wretched men and women such as we are, I don't believe He thought in terms of how little He should give, but *how much*. Our hearts should—*must*—be overflowing with thankfulness and gratitude for all our Father has given.

When I returned home from my trip, I received an added surprise. Those little buds were in full bloom, brightening my home with their extravagance…and a lingering fragrance of love.

STRONGHOLD

Take a few moments to read Mark 14:3-9. Jesus reminds us in Mark 14 that praise—extravagant, lavish, and profuse—comes before any request. There is nothing wasteful about loving praise. Take some moments right now and offer up a "sacrifice of praise" to the One who sacrificed so much for you.

COMING HOME TO GOD'S WORD

*So faith comes from hearing, and hearing by the
word of Christ.*

ROMANS 10:17

y husband Ken came home from a fishing trip
last Saturday afternoon and plopped contentedly
into his favorite chair. "This is great," he sighed.
"I've looked forward to coming home."

He'll never know how much that little comment
warmed my heart. I so much want our home to be a place
of refreshment for him, a place where he likes to spend his
time.

I think that's what Paul was talking about when he told
the Colossians, "Let the full richness of Christ's teaching
find its home among you" (3:16, Phillips). God intends
His Word to *dwell* within us, to make its home in us.
What a poignant way to put it. Think how well you
know your own home—or perhaps the home where you
grew up. Visualize its rooms and hallways, its closets and
cupboards. You know it like the back of your hand, don't
you? Which part of the roof leaks when it rains. The way
the dining room looks in the moonlight. The smell of
your old cedar chest.

Home. A place of familiarity and relaxation. A place to
build memories. The focus for so many of our hopes and
longings.

When Paul said, "Let the word of Christ dwell in you
richly," he was reminding us that Scripture should find a

home in our hearts, that we should live in its light. And, much like any other home, we should know it like the back of our hands. We should be able to place where most things are within its pages. We should go to God's Word because we prefer it—we're familiar with its commands and we relax in its promises.

I can visualize one dear old saint who has lived comfortably in the Word of God for seventy-five years. He can not only quote chapter after chapter of his Bible verbatim, he can tell you where individual verses appear on the pages! When it comes to the Bible, this man's at home.

Let God's Word live in you with all of its richness, promises, teaching, and direction. Let it be your retreat from a cynical, pressure-filled world. Let it make you rich in true wisdom.

Wherever life takes you, wherever your road leads, home can be as close as your heart.

STRONGHOLD

"But where do I begin?" you might ask. One of the best plans I know of is the Topical Memory System *published by the Navigators. I've used it and the plan has definitely helped (they're not paying me to say this, either). Or start by looking up "word" in a Bible concordance and see what the Word of God says about itself in passages like Proverbs 30:5-6; Jeremiah 23:28-32; John 1:14; Romans 10:16-17; Colossians 3:16; and Hebrews 4:12.*

LOVING OUR LITTLE CORNER

Live a life of love, just as Christ loved us.
EPHESIANS 5:2, NIV

When I was a little girl, my mother would take me to Grandmom's place on housecleaning days. As we began work on the kitchen, Mom would delegate one corner of the floor to me. Then I'd go to work scrubbing with my little sponge.

Mom didn't expect me to scrub the entire kitchen. That would have been overwhelming. But I did just fine with my corner.

As I grew older, I noticed the size of my "corner" gradually increasing. Finally, the time came when I was expected to clean the entire floor myself—along with the countertops and appliances, I might add.

Looking back, I'm glad my mother never expected me to houseclean to the DEGREE she did. But she *did* expect me to perform that chore in her same MANNER. I was expected to do a good job on the tiny piece of floor that was my responsibility. My little corner was supposed to shine.

That's very much the way God deals with us. There is no way I can obey to the same DEGREE that Jesus obeyed His Father. It would be overwhelming—demoralizing—if God expected me to sacrifice to the degree that He sacrificed. I can't. I can't love with the same intensity, the same strength as He. The thought of even trying fills me with despair.

Now granted, we may not be able to love to the same DEGREE as our heavenly Father. But we *can* love or obey or even sacrifice in the same MANNER as He. "Be imitators of God, therefore, as dearly loved children," Paul writes, "and live a life of love, just as Christ loved us and gave himself up for us" (Ephesians 5:1-2, NIV).

As we imitate our Father, then, we learn to love like Him. God loves the worthless...we are expected to love the worthless. God loves His enemies...we are expected to love our enemies. He sacrificed...we must sacrifice in the same manner.

So how are things in your corner of ministry today? Do all your efforts seem small compared to others? Don't worry about the degree of your love and sacrifice and service. That will come in time. Just concentrate on imitating your heavenly Father, on living life as Christ would live it through you. In the same way. In the same manner.

Make your little corner shine. Then watch it grow.

STRONGHOLD

Read Matthew 25:14-28 and be joyful about the day God will say to you, "Well done, good and faithful servant! You have been faithful with a few things; I will put you in charge of many things. Come and share your Master's happiness!" But wait a minute. Are you afraid of your little corner expanding and extending? Sound like too much responsibility? Take a closer look at Matthew 25:15.

PRECONCEIVED NOTIONS

For God so loved the world, that He gave His only begotten Son.

JOHN 3:16

hy do we get bored with the beautiful paintings we hang on our walls?

You know what I'm talking about. You position a painting in a certain room, and after a few weeks you're oblivious to it. It's as though the painting has become invisible. Mysteriously absorbed by the Masonite. Swallowed alive by the wallpaper.

Why is that?

The fault may not lie in the painting at all. It may lie with you, and with the way you view that piece of art. You may be simply "using" the painting. Using it to fill up the space on your wall. Using it to accent the color on your decorator couch. Some people treat paintings as launch pads for their own imaginations and emotional activities. They bring their own agendas to the artwork. They *do* things with the painting, rather than laying themselves open to see what the painting might do for them.

Appreciating a given work of art demands that we set aside our preconceptions, prejudices, and mental associations. That's why you see people in art museums sitting for long minutes in front of a Rembrandt. They allow the painting to speak to them.

The first demand any work of art makes upon us is to

surrender. We must look, and go on looking until we have seen exactly what is there. Only when our ideas about Rembrandt are set aside, can Rembrandt's ideas reach us.

That principle of art has taught me something about a principle of Scripture. So many of us come to a biblical passage with preconceived notions and expectations about what we think it ought to say to us. We treat the Bible as a launch pad for our own ideas or desires. We have no intention of *receiving* God's Word…only *using* it.

But the first demand the Bible makes on us as we read is to surrender. To lay aside our prejudices, agendas, and pet theories. To read and re-read until we see exactly what is being said.

Only when *our* ideas about the Lord Jesus are set aside, can His ideas reach us.

STRONGHOLD

A verse such as John 3:16 is probably very familiar territory to you. But it can still remain fresh. How? First, ask the Holy Spirit to help you. Then, read the verse slowly several times, each time placing special emphasis and thoughtful meditation on one word. "For GOD so loved the world…For God SO loved the world…For God so LOVED the world"…and so on. Prayerfully approach other favorite verses this way and begin to understand God's ideas for you—fresh and new!

THE HEART OF THE WINDOW

I am the way, and the truth, and the life;
no one comes to the Father, but through Me.

JOHN 14:6

Here it is the first of June and I just finished painting one of my premiere designs for the upcoming Christmas season. You heard me right—Christmas!

You see, I have to finish my paintings this far in advance to assure that they will be ready for the holiday season. And I'm really excited about this painting. It's painted to look like a stained glass window, with a figure of Mary holding baby Jesus. A king, one of the magi, kneels on one side of them, and a shepherd on the other.

My window is filled with symbols. The kneeling figures suggest the Child's destiny as both the Great Shepherd and the King of kings. The lamp at Mary's feet reminds us that He is the Light of the World. Christ is also called "the Rose of Sharon," and I painted a thorny bush of beautiful lavender roses cascading around Mary. A little lamb tucked against the shepherd foreshadows His role as the Lamb of God. The One sacrificed for my sin…and yours.

Pulling together all the elements and symbols in this picture was a real challenge. Different parts of the picture kept vying for attention—competing with one another. As the artist, it was my responsibility to give these symbols their proper relationship to one another so they would complement each other. It wasn't easy!

The king's robe, for instance, was very violet. Just too bright. So I had to keep putting on a coat of bright yellow paint, until it was finally subdued. In other portions of the painting the colors were too dull, too weak, and I had to keep brightening them—pulling them forward. I kept experimenting this way on all the parts of the picture, forcing them to cooperate with one another. Finally, all those parts obeyed.

When I looked at the painting, my eye went right to Jesus.

We're like that painting, aren't we? Instead of being unified as Christians, we vie with each other for special notice. We're all supposed to be adoring Jesus—like the figures kneeling in my window—and we end up muddling the message. Spoiling the focus.

God has to *force* us to cooperate with one another—pulling and pushing us into unity…until all the parts obey. When we finally come to that place, the message rings out loud and clear. Jesus—and Jesus only—is the center of attention.

STRONGHOLD

For an eye-opening account of just how destructive it can be when the parts of Christ's church start vying for attention, read 1 Corinthians 1:10-13. Continue on to 1 Corinthians 3 for the inside story. Ask yourself: How can I better cooperate with someone I've been competing against?

GOD'S POWER AND COMPASSION

'My house shall be called a house of prayer.'
But you have turned it into a thieves' kitchen!

MATTHEW 21:13, PHILLIPS

I t's easy to picture a kindly, loving Jesus. We've had lots of help on that score from religious artists down through the centuries. But do you find it a bit more challenging to visualize an angry—I mean violently angry—Jesus Christ?

The most notable instance is the scene with the moneychangers described in Matthew 21:10-13. This was not the "gentle Jesus, meek and mild." You can probably picture Him kicking over tables, overturning cash registers, grabbing those guys by the scruff of the neck and heaving them out the temple door onto their self-righteous backsides. No one, he asserted, was going to make *His* Father's house into a haven for con-men and rip-off artists. He meant business.

If I had been a moneychanger, I think I would have opted for a career change at that very moment—selling newspapers in Nazareth, baking bagels in Bethlehem, picking up gum wrappers in the park—anything to get away from the piercing gaze of this Man of Authority.

But if you want a surprise, catch the very next verse in Matthew 21. "And there in the Temple the blind and the lame came to him and he healed them" (v. 14).

Does that hit you the way it hit me? The Lord's angry shouts were still echoing from the temple walls. Coins were still rolling around on the pavement. But our Lord doesn't miss a beat. He immediately turns his attention to the blind and lame—releasing them from their physical bondage.

There is no room in Scripture for a one-sided view of our Lord. He points an angry, righteous finger at the hypocrites on one hand, yet reaches down to gently touch the need of the lowly with the other. He turns a face as hard as steel to the religious phonies yet smiles encouragement at those who reach out to Him in simple faith.

Do you identify with those weak, overlooked men and women in the far corner of the temple courtyard? Do you feel lonely today—perhaps ignored or devalued? Or maybe you're seeing a different face of God right now—the conviction of His anger with your sin and rebellion.

Remember this portrait of Jesus from the book of Matthew. He's powerful and He's going to deal with your sin. But He's also ready to forgive, heal your wounds, and offer you a fresh start.

STRONGHOLD

Notice in Romans 11:22 the two characteristics of God. Do you see a balance? Kindness is one characteristic; sternness might be considered its complement. Make a list of the complementary characteristics of God. Remember, there's no room for a one-sided view.

IS GOD PROUD?

Beware of practicing your righteousness before men.
MATTHEW 6:1

Dorothy's letter was full of sunlight. She penned such glowing words that I was, frankly, a little embarrassed. Then she made a curious comment. "Joni," she said, "God is surely proud of you and the way you've overcome your handicap."

I know she meant well, but I just couldn't let that sentence go by. Is God "proud" of us when we do something so simple as appropriate His grace? Somehow I can't imagine the Lord inserting His thumbs beneath His suspenders and glowing with pride over my obedience. After all, isn't obedience something you expect from servants?

On the other hand, I don't believe our Father in heaven is some frowning, straitlaced God who isn't moved by the sincere submission of His dearly loved children. I think of what the writer of Scripture said to the Hebrew believers: "God is not unjust; he will not forget your work and the love you have shown him as you have helped his people and continue to help them" (Hebrews 6:10, NIV). Jesus Himself said to the church in Ephesus: "I know your deeds, your hard work and your perseverance....You have persevered and have endured hardships for my name, and have not grown weary" (Revelation 2:2-3, NIV).

After all, you and I are intended for "the praise of His glory." And every time we step out in obedience, God must take pleasure in our actions, knowing they will result in honor and glory for His Son.

So what is it that makes me a little restless with the notion of God's pride in my response to the wheelchair?

It's simply this: I must never ever think I am doing God a great favor when I obey His Word or follow His commands. I am simply living the life God *expects* me to live. I am being conformed to Christ's image as He intends. I am experiencing the normal Christian life.

And the more I obey Him, the more I begin to grasp how far I am from His ultimate goal for my life. As Paul wrote in Philippians 3:12-14, I would rather look at how far I need to go, rather than at how far I have already come. In humility we can only forget what lies behind and run straight for the goal…the high calling of our God.

All of us have a long way to go.

STRONGHOLD

The person who feels he has done God a favor by obeying Him is described in Isaiah 29:13. Psalm 15 provides a clear snapshot of the one who obeys God out of humility and sincere submission. Which best describes you? Make it your prayer today to obey out of humility and submission.

THOSE "OTHER" PROMISES

We share in his sufferings in order that we may also share in his glory.

ROMANS 8:17, NIV

I t gives us a warm, secure feeling to sing "standing on the promises of Christ my King." Some of us have put God's promises on plaques above our fireplaces or stitched them into a needlepoint picture for the hallway. Such snug, comforting promises like…"I have come that you might have abundant life." Or, "He richly gives us all things." Or, "Ask and you shall receive." Or, "It will be done for you that your joy may be full."

We claim those promises as believers. We memorize them, meditate on them, make them our own. And rightly so. God intends us to enter into His promises.

But there's a catch. You can't pick and choose. God means for us to embrace *all His promises*. And not all His promises are snug and comfortable.

Especially the ones having to do with pain and hardship. No, we'd rather not "name 'n' claim" *those* promises. You won't find 2 Timothy 3:12 gracing many living room walls. You won't spy Acts 14:22 magnetized to many refrigerator doors.

Frankly, we'd rather circumvent the suffering. We make every effort to weed out all the discomfort in our lives. We consider trials and disciplines to be rude interruptions in our plans for an easy, comfortable life. We demand miracles of healing and are willing to believe all sorts of wild irrationalities in order to get what we want. We seek to escape the promise of hardship rather than to allow Him to work out His will in our lives through the experience.

I can recall a time when I used to think those promises were more like threats. *Oh, sure, the Bible promises a lot of hardship. Well, with friends like that, who needs enemies? If I break my neck at the age of seventeen, what in the world is going to happen when I reach twenty or thirty? If this is the way God is going to start out discipling me, then I might as well forget it!*

Yet I really wanted to be a disciple! I really wanted to follow Christ.

Do you see yourself in that contradiction? If we want to know Christ, a casual glance at the New Testament will tell us that God's Son was made perfect by suffering (Hebrews 2:10). And if the Christ of glory came to His glory only through suffering, how shall we know His glory any other way? If we want to know Him, and if we want to be made like Him, we can expect a few bumps and bruises along the way.

And that's a promise!

STRONGHOLD

John 16:33 offers a twofold promise: "In this world you will have trouble. But take heart! I have overcome the world." Why can we take heart despite the "other" promises made in these verses: Acts 14:22; Romans 8:17; James 1:2-3?

A RENDERING OF GOD

We…are being transformed into his likeness.

2 CORINTHIANS 3:18, NIV

little boy pulled out his crayons and sheet of paper one afternoon. Resting his hand on his chin, he thought a few minutes, then picked up a crayon and began sketching.

Noticing his intentness as he worked, his mother asked, "What are you drawing?"

"A picture of God," he replied without looking up.

His mother smiled. "But honey, no one knows what God looks like."

The boy put down his crayon and rubbed his hands together, still staring at his handiwork. "Well," he replied, "they will when I finish."

We smile at that little story. On one hand, we can understand the mother's point of view. John 1:18 tells us that no one has seen God at any time. God Himself told Moses, "You cannot see my face, for no one may see me and live" (Exodus 33:20, NIV).

But on the other hand, John 1:18 goes on to declare that God's only Son, Jesus Christ, *has made Him known.* Through His life and words and deeds, the Nazarene sketched an unerring illustration of His Father. He drew a picture so that we would have a clear idea of just who our Father in heaven really is. Jesus Christ is that perfect expression of the Father.

Much like the little boy, we are sketching an illustration for all to see—through our words and deeds, our everyday conversations, our attitudes and actions. Our lives should be a picture of what God looks like.

Intent as we are on living for Him, people will inevitably approach us and ask what we're doing. They'll be curious. Looking over our shoulders. Maybe even asking questions. Hopefully, they'll see a beautiful image in us—a clearer picture of just who God really is and what He's like.

No, He's not finished with us yet. But Paul assures us that as we fix our gaze on the Lord Jesus, we will resemble Him more and more with each passing day. "We, who with unveiled faces all reflect the Lord's glory," he writes, "are being transformed into his likeness with ever-increasing glory" (2 Corinthians 3:18, NIV).

So let's pick up our crayons and get to work! We've got a job to do. We've got to show a despairing, cynical world what God really looks like. If they didn't know before, maybe they'll know when we're finished...or, rather, when *He's* finished.

STRONGHOLD

People have painted pictures of the Lord Jesus throughout the centuries. But these capture only a stiff and motionless representation. God wants us to be "living pictures" of Him. Read 1 John 4:7-17 and think of ways you can color other people's impressions of God.

DON'T TOUCH THE TAR-BABY

*The spiritual ones among you should quietly set him back
on the right path.*
GALATIANS 6:1, PHILLIPS

Do you remember the Uncle Remus story of B'rer
Rabbit and the tar-baby? I can close my eyes and
see old tar-baby sitting on a log near the dear old
brier patch and B'rer Rabbit's front door. Someone had
plunked a hat on his head, stuck a pipe in his mouth, and
there tar-baby sat, waiting for an unsuspecting passer-by
to come along and give his hand a shake. And then that
poor somebody would be hopelessly stuck to that sticky,
icky black tar.

I once read an article in which the author gave fresh
meaning to that old story. He asked, "Do you know any
tar-babies—people better avoided, loaded down with
problems? Folks you'd rather not approach or come near?"

Any tar-babies in your church? I keep thinking of a
pretty tar-baby named Carol. Carol and her family are
members at a prominent evangelical church. She is an
outstanding senior at a Christian high school. Everyone
was stunned to hear that she had become pregnant. Her
school refused to let her continue her education. The
whole family is hurting, in desperate need of somebody
who will just mingle some tears with their tears—even in
their disgrace. But the church stands awkwardly by, shuf-
fling its feet, not knowing how to mix reproof and correc-
tion with love and encouragement.

Is it possible that we're so anxious to protect our spiritual reputation—or the reputation of our church—that we deliberately avoid the "contamination" of helping people in deep spiritual trouble? Do we think they will somehow tempt us to sin, too? Do we suppose that an "example" should be made of a wrong done? Do we fear that our loyalty to somebody in trouble tars us with their disgrace?

Paul had a better idea. He wrote some useful instructions to the church at Galatia in Galatians 6:1-5. Paul says that hurting, stumbling people are not tar-babies. To deliberately look the other way and give them a wide berth is not "discipline." It is spiritual snobbery—and a direct affront to the law of Christ.

Has someone come to your mind as you've read these words? Can you feel his shame and hurt? Take the apostles' advice. Restore that person…quietly, gently. Today. Mingle your tears with his. Touch his disgrace. Just as Jesus touched yours.

God forbid, but there may come a day when the tar-baby's shoe is on the other foot.

STRONGHOLD

Take five minutes right now to pray for a person in trouble, using Colossians 1:9-14 or James 5:13-16 as prayer guidelines.

Col 1:10 You wy live the kind of life that honors & pleases the Lord in every way.

Jam 5:16 Confess your sins to each other & pray for each other.

AGAINST YOU, YOU ONLY...

Against you, you only, have I sinned and done what is evil in your sight.

PSALM 51:4, NIV

I t hit me like a sudden shaft of sunlight piercing the clouds. I'd been reading Psalm 51 and came across the anguished words of David in verse 4.

I felt a pang as I whispered the words aloud. "Against you, you only..." How often did I really consider whether my sins, big or small, offended God? Wasn't my attention more on myself, or on those I might have offended, than it was on the Lord?

Perhaps I don't feel as though I've sinned against God when it involves small things that I can sweep under the carpet of my conscience. Somewhere I've come up with this idea that God is there to handle the big things—the major struggles with the big temptations—but it's up to me and my self-control to deal with the little things.

I have a feeling quite a few people handle sin in much the same way. Our problem is that our attitude toward sin is more *self-centered* than God-centered.

Jerry Bridges, in his book *The Pursuit of Holiness,* agrees: "We are more concerned about our victory over sin than we are about the fact that our sins grieve the heart of God. We cannot tolerate failure in our struggle with sin chiefly because we are success-oriented, not because we know it is offensive to God."

Now you might say that "small" sins of disobedience or

neglect don't really offend God, that He is quite content to have you sweep little things under the carpet. Not so. Perhaps half of the problem is that we do not take sin seriously enough—that we have mentally categorized sins into those which are unacceptable and those which may be tolerated.

When you come right down to it, we never see sin in its true perspective until we see all of it lined up against a holy God. All of our sin drove the nails into Jesus' hands and feet. All of our sin caused the Father's white-hot wrath to fall across His shoulders.

Big things...or eensy, weensy, small things...we must understand that in all things it is wise to say with the psalmist, "Against you, you only, have I sinned, Lord."

STRONGHOLD

Read 2 Samuel 11 to get an inside look at the way David kept trying to sweep his sin under the carpet. What "little sins" frequently go unconfessed and unrepented in your life? Present them in confession before God.

KEEPING GOD'S ATTENTION

*The LORD will watch over your coming and going both
now and forevermore.*

PSALM 121:8, NIV

T here's nothing more frustrating than trying to
keep someone's attention. I went through that
game as an immature teenager, desperately seeking to impress the captain of the football team from our
neighboring high school.

I vividly recall those ridiculous mental gymnastics I
went through…trying to dress right…combing my hair
just so…losing those few extra inches around my
waist…working so hard to impress…striving to pique his
interest with my witty conversation. I felt that his fond-
ness for me waxed and waned according to how clever
and cool my overtures were.

I'm reminded of that frenzied high school relationship
every time I catch myself trying to keep God's attention.
Have you ever thought of it in those terms? When illness
comes, when anxiety threatens, when conflict disturbs our
friendships, we may conclude that God has become bored
looking after us and has shifted His attention to a more
"exciting" Christian.

*"Look over there, archangel Gabriel. Now, that young
woman has possibilities. She's a climber. So responsive!
So disciplined and faithful! On her way up in the
kingdom. Too bad about Joni. I think we've invested
more than enough time and energy in her for a while."*

If you ever find yourself thinking thoughts like these, run, don't walk, to the book of Psalms. Get alone for a few uninterrupted minutes with Psalm 121. Open your heart and let the Spirit of God bring those words home to you in a very personal way. It won't be long before those feelings of discouragement and inner turmoil begin to fade like a bad dream.

Down in a valley, in desperate need of encouragement, the psalmist looks all around him—north, south, east, and west. From where will his help come? Only from the Lord, the very creator of those intimidating mountains and hills that surround him (vv. 1-2). With his eyes focused on this mighty source of strength, the singer's spirit begins to bubble over with assurance.

This caring, concerned God, he tells us, "will not let your foot slip." Twenty-four hours every day, seven days a week, He will keep watch over you. He is a shade to you through long, weary days and a guardian through the darkest of nights (vv. 3- 6).

You already have God's attention and you will never lose it. The real question is, how will He keep yours?

STRONGHOLD

As you read Psalm 121, insert your own name in each verse, just to see how personally God involves Himself with your life's details.

GLORY: THE EVERYDAY WORD

We all...are being transformed into the same image from glory to glory.

2 CORINTHIANS 3:18

6 lory." That's one of those lofty, in-the-clouds words, isn't it? Difficult to visualize. Hard to get in focus. The meaning is either so heavy we can't keep a grip on it—or so high above our heads that we can't even reach it.

At one time I felt "glory" must mean some kind of cosmic brilliance or blinding light. Images of long-ago Bethlehem would play on the screen of my mind, with magnificent heavenly beings shouldering back the night and shouting out, "Glory to God in the highest!"

In recent days, however, I've learned that "glory" comes closer to home than that. Much closer. Glory, I've learned, is what God is all about. His essential being. Whenever you talk about His character or attributes—like holiness, love, compassion, justice, truth, or mercy—that's God's glory. And when He reveals Himself in any of those qualities, we say He is "glorifying Himself."

In times past, He revealed those qualities in both places and people. He still does.

Not long ago I entered a friend's home and immediately sensed the glory of God. No, that impression was not based on some heebie-jeebie feeling or super-spiritual instinct. Yet there was a peace and orderliness that pervaded that home. Although the kids were normal, active youngsters, everyone's activity seemed to dovetail together, creating the impression that the home had direction, that the kids really cared about each other, that the parents put love into action. We didn't even spend much time talking about the Bible or praying together. Yet we laughed. And really heard each other. And opened our hearts like family members.

After dinner I left that home refreshed. It was a place where God's essential being was on display. His kindness, His love, His justice. It was filled with God's glory.

So how can you and I glorify God? It happens every time we reveal His attributes in the course of our daily lives. Every time we share the good news of Christ with another. Every time we reflect patience in the middle of an upsetting problem. Every time we smile from the heart or offer an encouraging word. Whenever we display God's character, we are displaying His glory.

Far from being some spacey concept out of a theology text, glory is as close as our next breath, as real as a smile on a dark day, as warm as the clasp of a caring hand.

STRONGHOLD

Look at 2 Corinthians 3:12-18, especially the last verse. Have you ever considered that you are a mirror which reflects the glory of the Lord? When are people best able to see the Lord glorified in your life?

GOD OF THE LITTLE THINGS

Just as a father has compassion on his children,
So the LORD has compassion on those who fear Him.

PSALM 103:13

I Is God concerned about the details of your life? Does He care about the "little things"?

Piles of dishes need to be done. The typewriter runs out of ribbon. The washer leaks a big soapy puddle on the floor—and you've got people coming in an hour. Little things.

Nobody else seems to notice or pay that much mind...so why should God? After all, isn't He the God of the BIG things? Isn't He the One who spoke swirling galaxies into the vast frontiers of space, who measured the waters in the hollow of His hand and calculated the dust of the earth (Isaiah 40:12)?

Why should this great, awesome God notice the tears that came to my eyes this morning at breakfast—when no one else noticed? Why should the Creator of the universe care about the worries that kept me awake until two in the morning? Why should the mighty Sovereign of eternity be concerned about the fact that I'm late for an appointment and can't find a parking place?

Sure, the Bible says He has compassion for His people. But isn't that sort of a "general" compassion for mankind? Isn't that an arms-length kind of compassion? Like a multimillionaire might feel when he writes out a check for an anonymous poor child living on the other side of the world.

Just how intimately is God involved in our small, petty problems? David in Psalm 103:6-14 says He has the compassion of a father.

I remember my father having a kind of intimate, heartfelt compassion with me. Often when my dad would be busy at his easel, I'd sit on the floor at his side with my crayons and coloring book. Even though he was intent on his work, he'd look down at me and smile. And sometimes he'd set his brushes aside, reach down, and lift me into his lap. Then he'd fix my hand on one of his brushes and enfold his larger, stronger hand around mine. Ever so gently, he would guide my hand and the brush, and I would watch in amazement as, together, we made something beautiful. Even these many years later, I find myself warmed by his compassion for me.

This is the kind of love our God has for us. Fatherlove. The kind, gentle compassion of a dad who deeply cares for his sons and daughters. Maybe you never had a dad like that…but you do have such a Father.

Let God's big hand close gently over yours. With His help, even the discouraging scribbles of your life can become a masterpiece. Nothing would delight a father's heart more.

STRONGHOLD

Does God care about your little annoyances? Just in case you doubt, read 2 Kings 6:1-7 and 1 Peter 5:6-7.

GOD'S SECRETS

The LORD confides in those who fear him.
PSALM 25:14, NIV

Can I tell you a secret? That's something I would very likely do if you and I became close friends. I'm a people person, and it just comes naturally to confide in a friend, seek sympathy when I'm hurt, or look for approval if I complete a painting I'm especially pleased with.

Almost everybody engages in those sorts of social bonds. Our trustfulness, our eagerness to find some ear for our most sacred secrets demonstrates that we're people-dependent. The satisfaction we find in sharing our hopes and cares and wrongs with those who care about us is a sign we are finite and frail…so very, very human.

God, on the other hand, is a mystery. He holds back many things to remind us of His unapproachable majesty and perfection. Unlike us, He often remains silent. A silence that tells us He is totally self-sufficient. If He so chooses, God can accomplish all of His desire without the slightest cooperation of a single one of us. "Whom did the LORD consult to enlighten him, and who taught him the right way?" asks the prophet Isaiah (Isaiah 40:14, NIV).

The answer, of course, is no one.

But here's the marvel. Although God is totally self-sufficient, He *chooses* to involve Himself in our lives. There's a little verse in Psalm 25 which astounds me every time I think of it. "The LORD confides in those who fear him; he makes his covenant known to them" (v.14, NIV).

God doesn't need little old me. He certainly doesn't require my advice. He doesn't need my attention, emotional support, or listening ear. He can go about His business as though I never existed. (He seemed to manage just fine before I was born.) It is only by His unbelievable grace that He calls my simple labor an actual service to Himself. He permits, and even solicits, my help. And to think He would even whisper the secrets of His heart in my ear!

But here's the catch. Usually we reserve our secrets and confidences for those with whom we are especially buddy-buddy. Not so with God. God reserves intimacies for those who *fear* Him. Those who hold Him in awe and deep respect. Those who revere His name.

I'm overwhelmed at His great glory, His total self-sufficiency, His holiness and completeness. But I'm even more overwhelmed when I consider that God, by His own choice, makes His covenants known to you and me. Insecure, frail, stumbling you and me.

That's a secret I can hardly keep to myself.

STRONGHOLD

Has God taken you into His confidence lately? If so, take a moment to praise Him. If not, remember this: when you fear the Lord, it's like cupping your ear so you may hear Him!

GOD'S HUMILITY

*He humbled Himself by becoming obedient to the
point of death.*

PHILIPPIANS 2:8

When I ponder the marvelous attributes of my
God, there's always one quality which moves me
above all the rest. The humility of our Savior.

Contrasted against His glory and greatness as the
Creator of the universe, His humility is all the more strik-
ing. Scripture tells us that through Christ "all things were
created: things in heaven and on earth, visible and invisible,
whether thrones or powers or rulers or authorities; all
things were created by him and for him. He is before all
things, and in him all things hold together....For God
was pleased to have all his fullness dwell in him"
(Colossians 1:16-17, 19, NIV).

Now ponder, through this poem, the *humility* of Jesus.

The Hands that shaped the flaming spheres
        and set them spinning, vast light years
        away from Planet Earth,
have laid aside the Robes of State,
donned human likeness by the great
        indignity of birth.
The hands, responsive to Love's Plan,
that formed the God-reflector, Man,
        of dust and destiny,
outstretched—by Man's fierce hate impaled—

wrought life anew, Love's Plan unveiled
　　upon Golgotha's Tree.

The Hands that found it nothing strange
to pucker up a mountain range
　　or ladle out a sea,
that balance Nature's systems still,
and shape all History to His will,
　　hold, and are molding, me![3]

For me, the supreme demonstration of the nature and
character of our great God was when He laid aside His
divine splendor, took upon Himself the form of a servant,
and died a martyr's death for us. Since God has done *that*,
surely He has proven His intentions.

STRONGHOLD

Open your Bible to 2 Corinthians 8:9 and Philippians 2:1-11.
Spend at least five minutes today pondering what the Lord
Jesus gave up to become your Savior.

---

3. Marion Donaldson, " His Hands," copyright 1972. Used by permission.

IN THE FAMILY

He is not ashamed to call them brethren.

HEBREWS 2:11

You've heard the phrase, "Blood is thicker than water." When I was a girl, an expression like that would have sounded gross. But I instinctively understood its meaning. For even though I loved my friends, there was nobody who could match the importance of my three older sisters.

Sure, we had our share of scuffles—which occasionally erupted into screaming, full-scale, hand-to-hand combat. Just routine sibling rivalry, right?

Ah, but as much as I squared off with my sisters, I was always glad to be paired off with them. I took special pride in being the youngest of four girls. I loved posing for photographs with them. Inwardly, I was tickled with their achievements. And I glowed with pleasure when they'd say something nice about me. Their opinions meant much more than even my best friend's.

There's something wonderful about sharing the same genetics with another person—the same parents, roots, background, memories, history, and, in a sense, flesh and blood.

I was reminded of that "blood-is-thicker" expression just recently as I read in the book of John. Throughout the course of His life on earth, the Lord Jesus had special names for those who followed Him. He called them His servants, His sheep, or His beloved. He seemed to have special nicknames for at least several of them. At the last supper, He must have encouraged His men mightily when He named them "friends" (see John 15:14-15).

It wasn't until after His resurrection, however, that Christ referred to His disciples as His brothers. One of the first things Jesus said after He rose from the dead was, "Mary, go to My brothers and tell them that I am returning to My Father and your Father."

Even though He was as close as a good friend could be to the men and women who followed Him through His earthly ministry, He couldn't call them blood relatives until after He paid the penalty for sin and welcomed them into the family. Christ's death and resurrection opened the door for men and women to share the same genes, so to speak, with the Son of God. To share the same Father and family.

That thought stirs me so! What must Jesus have felt to utter for the first time the word, brothers to us?

Blood is thicker than water. And if you have found salvation through Jesus Christ, you can never be an only child. You're in the family of Jesus.

STRONGHOLD

How does your big Brother, the Lord Jesus, feel about naming you as one of the family? Flip to Hebrews 2:5-18 and take a little pride in the way Jesus speaks of His relationship to you.

GRACE: FRESH DAILY

Give us this day our daily bread.
MATTHEW 6:11

ot long ago I was looking through a *National Geographic* magazine and came across an article on the Sinai wilderness. Page after page showed photos of a dry wasteland. Vegetation amounted to a few scrub bushes here and there and an occasional lonely palm.

It prompted me to think about the forty years the nation Israel wandered in the wilderness after the exodus from Egypt. The Bible tells us that the main staple of their diet during that time was a flaky foodstuff called "manna."

They ate that stuff for forty years. Can you imagine? They must have outdone Julia Child in thinking of 101 ways to make manna taste different. Yet it was food. It was life. And it was necessary for them to gather it fresh every morning before it could melt away in the heat of the noonday sun.

A few years ago I also found myself in a wilderness. I wasn't camping in Death Valley or trekking across the Utah salt flats. I was in bed...for three long months...with a pressure sore that refused to heal.

There were times during that twelve-week stay in bed that I wondered how I would continue. I'd get depressed just thinking about the remaining weeks I needed to stay out of my wheelchair. Plans were interrupted, paintings were postponed, and I discovered that there are only so many books, tapes, or TV programs you can endure for that length of time flat on your back.

It's been said that grace is the desire and the power to do God's will. Well, I lacked both. It was clear that this grace, this gift, was going to have to come from God. And as a gift, it's something for which I had to ask.

James tells us the asking must be done in humility. "God opposes the proud," he writes, "but gives grace to the humble" (4:6, NIV). At that point I wasn't having trouble with pride. I had come to a place where I was broken, humbled, even humiliated by my lack of ability. Yet my mind was locked up with worry over the future.

Numb with anxiety, I finally came across verses from Lamentations 3 which unlocked my spirit: "For His compassions never fail. They are new every morning" (vv. 22-23). In other words, the grace God gives you today is sufficient *for today only.* Just like the Israelites, I had to wake up in the morning, go out, and gather a day's supply. It was no good trying to stockpile grace for the long, hungry days ahead.

Grace, like manna, can't be stored. It is "new every morning."

STRONGHOLD

Look more closely at Philippians 2:12-13 and James 4:6-10. What do we call that work of God in our life? You guessed it—grace.

4:7 Submit yourself then to God. Resist the devil, and He will flee from you.

DYING OF THIRST

Whoever drinks of the water that I shall give him shall never thirst.

JOHN 4:14

J ohan is young, tall, blond, and Dutch. Gifted and handsome, Johan could have carved out a comfortable youth ministry in his native Netherlands—or most anywhere in the world, for that matter.

Comfort, however, isn't one of Johan's major goals. He chose to take the gospel of Christ to the bedouins and nomads near Israel's desolate Sinai desert. A forgotten people in one of the most desolate corners of the world.

Johan works by an oasis near the sea, attracting travelers and bedouins by offering hot meals, clothing, and first aid. Following this hospitality, he tells Bible stories and gives a simple testimony of his faith in the One who walked the same sandy waste, two thousand years ago. He has a message to offer—and considers it every bit as valuable as the life-giving water he ladles out to his guests. From the bedouins, Johan learned it is considered worse than murder if you know of a water source and yet neglect to tell your fellow man.

Not many among us will ever proclaim salvation to desert nomads. But all around us, no matter where we reside or work, there are thirsty men and women. The neighbor down the street, the man at the service station, the boy who carries our groceries, the secretary who types and files, or even the distant aunt who occasionally comes by for visits. If these people don't know Christ, they're going to die of thirst.

In John 4, Jesus had a conversation with a thirsty woman. It was a hot, dry day in a town near the desert. Sitting on the edge of an ancient well, He talked to the woman about two kinds of thirst: the immediate, physical sort, and a deeper, more profound thirst of the soul. "Everyone who drinks of this water shall thirst again;" He told her, "but whoever drinks of the water that I shall give him shall never thirst; but the water that I shall give him shall become in him a well of water springing up to eternal life" (vv. 13-14).

The woman left her waterpot unfilled and hurried back into the city. Yet her thirst was quenched that day as never before. She had found a deeper well. She had found the Source of living water and didn't waste a moment in telling everyone in town.

Do you know the Source of living water? If you do, please don't withhold a drink from somebody who is thirsty.

It's not just a matter of hospitality. It's a matter of life and death.

STRONGHOLD

Read John 7:37-39, thinking about the climate in which these people lived. Why do you think Jesus used the analogy of a river instead of a lake or pool or some other body of water?

FINGERS OF LOVE

You are the body of Christ.
1 CORINTHIANS 12:27, NIV

Can you hear the voice, the words—somewhere in your memory? "I know it hurts...but remember, God screens the suffering that comes into your life. He filters it through fingers of love, giving you only that which works for your good and will point you toward Him."

Have words like those, spoken with kindness and deep concern, ever sifted down and settled into your mind—perhaps through a cloud of pain or grief? They are good words, and true. It's an incalculable comfort to know that God won't let trials pour on top of us like sand slipping carelessly through His fingers.

But let's take that hopeful thought a quantum leap further. True, God filters everything through His fingers. But did you ever stop to consider *that you are one of His fingers?*

Paul states it point blank in 1 Corinthians 12:12-27. We are His body. We make up the hands and the feet and the eyes and the ears—and fingers, too. Talk about feeling special and close to Him! That's as close as you can get. The Lord Jesus is our head, and you and I make up His body here on earth. There could be no more intimate linkage.

God would never do anything to harm His body. What foolishness to suggest He would do Himself purposeful and deliberate injury. Yet some of us seem to think just that. It shows in our reactions and attitudes. Embittered, thoughtless reactions tell the world we don't trust God when He allows pain or problems to touch us. In a way, when we grumble and complain against the hardships, we are saying that God is thoughtlessly harming His own body.

To correct that kind of thinking, we need to see ourselves intimately linked, actual members of Christ's body—a body God would never do anything to harm. The Spirit of God can teach us this truth, when we are ready to listen.

Our Father doesn't simply filter our sorrows and setbacks through His fingers, we *are* those fingers. Don't allow thoughtless voices or the Enemy himself tell you differently!

STRONGHOLD

If God filters trials and disappointments through His fingers, and we are those fingers, it gives us real responsibility toward one another. What can you do—as the very fingers of Jesus Christ—to protect, to push away the harm, to wipe away the tears, to hold a hand, or clasp a shoulder of someone who is discouraged?

TAKING THE INITIATIVE

We love, because He first loved us.

1 JOHN 4:19

I t's a good thing I can't knot my hands into a fist. Because if I could, I'd probably punch things when I get mad. Ken, for instance. Wait—don't take me too seriously. I doubt our disagreements would ever get that furious. But my husband and I are like every other couple you meet. We argue...carefully observing a couple of basic rules, like letting the other person have his say without interrupting and promising to listen.

Yet even when we argue with the best of intentions, we *still* come up against barricades. Attitudinal roadblocks. I get stubborn and refuse to compromise. Or I get resentful because I feel like I have to give in more than *he* does in order to resolve the conflict.

When Ken and I reach one of those impasses, we sometimes sit for long minutes in belligerent silence. And as I sit there, I secretly resent the demands of marriage. I find I have a reluctance to give away any more than absolutely necessary. I feel a temptation to pull back from the full intensity of my relationship with Ken and settle for the "basic requirements."

But in the middle of all that stubbornness, Ken is usually the first to break the silence and take the initiative. Unaccountably, he will begin to show forgiveness and love. That *shocks* me. It catches me up short. Ken doesn't wait around until I am repentant or promise to change my ways. He loves me...argumentative person that I sometimes am. And that makes me love him all the more right back.

That's exactly what God has done for us. The Father didn't wait around until He had an apology before He sent Jesus. He took the initiative. He didn't fold his arms and tap His foot, waiting until we "came around," until we shaped up and changed our ways.

No, God caught us up short in that "while we were yet sinners, Christ died for us." I can't resist such love. It amazes me that the Lord loved me long before I promised to give Him my life or change my ways. The result is just as the apostle John predicted: I find that I love Jesus Christ "because He first loved us."

That's called taking the initiative. It's not only a principle God uses with us, it's also a plan of action we, in turn, need to implement with each member of our family...and God's family.

Don't sit there and stew in your stubbornness. If you want to heal what's hurting, either in your life or in the life of another, take the initiative. Like Christ.

STRONGHOLD

Are you aware of a hurt that could be healed if only you would take the initiative? What does Matthew 5:21-24 indicate about the practice of waiting for the other person to "come around"?

"BUT I'M SO SMALL..."

Where were you when I laid the foundation of the earth!

JOB 38:4

L ast week Ken and I pitched a tent underneath some tall, straight Sequoias near a mountain creek flowing swiftly with melted snow from the high Sierras. Mornings were crisp—almost cold—and that made the aroma of fresh mountain trout sizzling on the breakfast campfire smell even better.

One morning we rented a boat on a lake laden with trout. The scenery was enough to suck the breath out of your lungs. It made me feel so small, drifting around in that little rowboat, surrounded by soaring mountain peaks, wide blue water, and blustery winds. Like being in some vast cathedral. I felt like whispering.

I thought of Job as we watched those high mountain glaciers and drifted in the morning stillness. He, too, must have felt so very small that day when the Almighty came down to question him about laying the foundations of the earth, forming the ice and snow, counting the clouds, and directing the eagles (Job 38 and 39).

Yes, the mountains, the snow, the hawks and eagles, the clouds and wind all have a way of making me feel almost insignificant as I see the measureless greatness of God. But before I begin to think of myself as a tiny speck in God's fathomless universe, there is another side of the story to consider.

As marvelous as those wonders are, God stripped Himself of all His divine trappings and humbled Himself...to save me. As Paul wrote in Philippians 2:5-9, Christ became small in the eyes of the world...He became insignificant in the sight of men...He even made Himself lower than the angels...for me. To lift me up.

Have you been overshadowed by some larger-than-life realities around you lately? Are there times when you cringe with Job, thinking that you are so small, so...so nothing? Please don't stop there. Don't be overwhelmed. Recognize that this same God who towers around you also humbled Himself and became a man. He lived and died and came out of that grave for you. To lift you up.

There's nothing small or insignificant about that.

STRONGHOLD

Do something small today. Listen in on a conversation between two grade schoolers. Read a chapter from Little House on the Prairie. *Wind up a music box and hum along with the tune. Then read the account in Matthew 19:13-14 of Jesus, the Creator of the universe, enjoying time and small talk with children. Was anyone too small in His eyes?*

DUBIOUS ROOTS

But My righteousness shall be forever,
And My salvation to all generations.

ISAIAH 51:8

not long ago my sisters and I followed an intriguing branch of the Eareckson family tree. On a crisp morning in early winter, we crossed Chesapeake Bay Bridge and found the original Eareckson homestead and the little family graveyard nearby. Kathy poked around the base of a large, spreading oak tree, pushing aside the ivy and tangled brush until she struck rock. There it was—a moss-covered stone with a crudely chiseled name: BENJAMIN EARECKSON. And then another, ELIZABETH EARECKSON. We were thrilled—you'd have thought we'd found gold.

On our way back to Baltimore, we invented stories about Benjamin and Elizabeth. Pushing back the frontier. Planting the Eareckson banner in the American soil. They were probably early settlers from Scandinavia. Farmers, perhaps. Or maybe fishermen, since their home was on the edge of a creek leading to the Bay. They must have made friends with the Indians. Their sons probably went to Baltimore and became shipbuilders, or went to Washington and became lawyers. I was bursting with pride and I didn't even know those people.

My pride later deflated when I happened to look through a detailed record of our family history. There I noticed that Benjamin not only kept slaves but willed them to his son. A postscript added that the Eareckson family dealt kindly with their slaves, but I was hurt nonetheless.

I wonder how the Lord Jesus felt about His human ancestry. A careful study reveals a few rather remarkable characters up in the limbs of His family tree. Kings and poets. Saints and sinners. Jews and Gentiles.

Look, for example, at four women mentioned in His genealogy: Tamar, Rahab, Ruth, and Bathsheba—all in need of forgiveness. The presence of these women in the genealogy of Jesus speaks of the extent of God's mercy. It shows how great God's forgiveness really is, how wide His grace. God identified with forgiven sinners, even to the point of including them in His Son's human ancestry.

What does that say to you and me? You may feel like an outcast, an outsider. You may feel shame over your family background. You may still ache over the consequences of past sins and failures. Could God's mercy really be available to you? Could He actually love you and use your life for His glory?

No matter who you are, where you've been, or what you've done, you can be a member of God's royal family. And that…is grace.

STRONGHOLD

To appreciate the extent of God's mercy, read about the four women in the genealogy of Jesus—Genesis 38:6-26; Joshua 2:1-21; Ruth 1-4; and 2 Samuel 11:2-5.

WASHING

*If we confess our sins, He is faithful and righteous
to forgive us our sins and to cleanse us from
all unrighteousness.*

1 JOHN 1:9

The young wife tenderly leaned over her husband in the wheelchair. Her husband, severely brain damaged as a result of an automobile accident, lifted his head slightly and smiled.

"I used to have a hard time accepting Bob's injury," she said, smiling as she looked at him. "And the hardest part was bathing my husband. He would stand in the shower and hold onto the towel rack while I scrubbed his back. All the while my tears mingled with the running water. My big, strong, handsome husband...now he couldn't do for me; I had to do for him. Even to the point of washing him.

"But all that changed when I realized that Jesus did the same—no, I take that back. He did *much more* when He washed me of the dirt and filth in my own life. Now I count it a privilege to give Bob a bath."

As I listened to this woman's story, I was reminded that we're washed every day as believers.

In John 13, the Lord got on His hands and knees and washed the dirty feet of His own disciples.

In Psalm 51 David pled with God to wash him.

I wonder if David had always had that attitude. I wonder if he ever felt a reluctance about being bathed by somebody else even if that somebody was God. There came a day, however, when King David had no hesitations. He was so soiled, so thoroughly stained by sin and guilt, that he fell from his throne and on bended knees cried out to God for cleansing.

The young woman with the brain-damaged husband began to change her attitude toward washing as she realized what her Lord was doing for her every day. God was cleansing away a great deal more dirt and filth from her life than she ever had to face when approaching her husband with a washcloth in hand.

Now, you may not be in a nursing home having to go through bed baths every day. You may not be in bed or ill while others take care of those very intimate needs. But you may be in need of someone who can give you a real cleansing.

If your feet are dirty or your hands are soiled from the everyday contact with this world, let God wash you, making you whiter than snow, and let Him create in you a clean heart.

STRONGHOLD

Washing His disciples' feet was the last act of service Jesus performed before He went to the cross. Read about it in John 13:1-17 and notice our Lord's words in verses 14-17. How can you "wash the feet" of a friend or family member? What should your attitude be?

THRESHING

Tribulation brings about perseverance.
ROMANS 5:3

My friend Bev took a unique vacation recently. Shunning Disneyland and the High Sierras, she and her husband and kids drove back to the family farm in North Dakota to help with the wheat harvest. Since I don't know much about wheat, I asked her to describe just what goes on at harvest. Bev recounted how the big combines come lumbering through the fields, raking the furrows of freshly cut wheat into the machine. The combine head, which resembles a rotating blade, then beats or *threshes* the stalks of wheat. The ripe grain is shaken loose and sucked into a large bin at the back of the combine. What's left, the straw and chaff, is spit back onto the ground, fodder for the next gust of prairie wind.

Since my conversation with Bev, I've learned that the biblical word *tribulation* has its root meaning in the word "thresh." What I've just described to you, believe it or not, is a process that applies to believers as well as wheat. Have a few of those big combines lumbered across the field toward you within the past year...perhaps within the past *week?*

Tribulations. Those big unavoidable trials that threaten to cut you down and beat you back and forth. Being threshed is never easy. Never pleasant. But Paul in Romans 5 tells us that tribulation brings about perseverance and perseverance yields a crop of "proven character" (v.4).

God is after something precious in your soul. Just like that North Dakota farmer, He's after a harvest...the golden grain of patience, perseverance, and strong character. And how is that grain harvested? Only through threshing...through tribulation. The farmer doesn't thresh weeds, does he? He wouldn't waste his time. He threshes the wheat which yields grain from the chaff. That priceless, blessed grain.

I know it's hard to picture "results" or the "yield" when you're going through so much testing. It's hard to imagine how God might be pleased or how you might be benefited. But splendid spiritual grain is to be found only in the lives of those with noble character—character gleaned through threshing.

Somehow that makes the beating and the flailing of a threshing trial worthwhile.

STRONGHOLD

Read Romans 5:1-5 and ask yourself this: What wonderful benefit grows out of "proven character"? As you come before your Lord in prayer today, ask Him to help you keep the perspective of these verses as pressures and problems enter your life in the coming week.

INSIDE PAIN

Cast all your anxiety on him because he cares for you.

1 PETER 5:7, NIV

Which pain is worse, physical or emotional?
Physical pain can almost be measured by degrees. Some have developed a remarkably high pain tolerance. Others can sometimes succeed at pushing physical pain right out of their thoughts by crowding their time and attention with other matters. If worse comes to worse, certain pain medications can block insistent pain messages.

But *inside* suffering…ah, that's a different matter. Mental anguish, resentment, bitterness, or even dryness of soul can hound us. And it isn't so easy to put those feelings behind us.

I think God permits this kind of inner anguish for a good reason. Physical hurt is almost outside of us, something we can drive from our thoughts. But inside pain is *within* our thoughts and forces us to cope with the problem. God may allow it because He knows this kind of suffering can be more purifying than any other kind of pain. We're forced to face it and deal with the situation at hand. If I'm hurting because of an argument with my husband or a disagreement with a friend at work, I'm miserable. Anxiety nags me and compels me to do something.

God says that inside anguish can be purifying. In 2 Corinthians 10:5, we're told that we can take captive every thought and make it obedient to Christ. What a promise! The anxiety, the worry, even the resentment or spiritual dryness can be used to make us deal with the issue at hand. And that means obedience.

Perhaps today you're feeling some inner hurt that refuses to be blocked out or forgotten. If the pain is due to a situation over which you no longer have control, commit it to the Lord right now in prayer. Don't carry it alone. If, on the other hand, the pain is a reminder of unconfessed sin, an unresolved conflict, or an unrepentant attitude, then get to the root of the problem. Deal with it. Don't languish another minute in your mental suffering. Not when you don't need to.

Only Jesus Christ can offer a cleansed heart and a clear conscience. "Peace I leave with you; my peace I give you. I do not give to you as the world gives. Do not let your hearts be troubled" (John 14:27, NIV).

STRONGHOLD

There is One who can enter your pain. The solitary Man, a man of sorrows who was acquainted with grief. When pain knocks on your door in the coming days, read again 2 Corinthians 10:5-7 and 1 Peter 5:6-11.

SEEK GOD'S FACE

*If my people…will humble themselves and…seek my face
and turn from their wicked ways.*

2 CHRONICLES 7:14, NIV

hen I was little, one day I secretly opened a small chest that belonged to my mother and took out her diary. I don't remember if I was even old enough to read—and I certainly can't recall having learned anything shocking about my mom. But I do remember that panicky sense of excitement as I hid behind the living room piano and delicately turned each page as though it were forbidden treasure.

After finishing, I carefully placed the diary back into the chest, situating it just so. I went out to play, the whole time thinking of my mother's diary…and feeling worse and worse about seeing her at dinnertime.

Mom rang the dinner bell at the back door, and we kids came running. I busily filled the supper table with a lot of anxious chatter, trying hard to act normal.

Finally Mom asked what the matter was. And you know something? I couldn't look her in the face. She'd catch my eyes for a moment, and then I'd quickly look down at my plate. Guilt prevented me from looking straight at my mother and answering her questions.

That little story is repeated in the lives of thousands of children and millions of adults. Looking another straight in the eyes has always been a test of truthfulness.

God knows that. In 2 Chronicles 7:14, He says, "If my

people, who are called by my name, will humble themselves and pray and seek my face and turn from their wicked ways, then will I hear from heaven and will forgive their sin and will heal their land" (NIV).

How I love that verse. But especially the part about seeking God's face. Just as I had to make things right with my mom before I could have eye-to-eye contact with her, I have learned that God wants me to seek His face. He desires to have eye-to-eye contact with me—transparent, truthful, lacking any guilt, guile, or sin. But that means confessing sin—my responsibility. No use filling my prayers with a lot of anxious chatter, trying to fake it with the Lord or lie to myself.

If you have a hard time gazing straight into the face of the Lord today, then you know you've got some confessing to do. God wants you to seek His face. There's nothing like eye-to-eye contact with our loving Father.

STRONGHOLD

Try looking up these five "face" verses—Psalm 27:7-9, Psalm 31:15-16, and Psalm 67:1-2, Psalm 104:27-30, and Psalm 143:7-9—and then top it off with that joyful reminder in 1 John 3:2-3. One day we shall see Him face to face!

MARY...OR MARTHA?

Jesus loved Martha and her sister and Lazarus.
JOHN 11:5, NIV

No doubt they made up a very ordinary family. Like most families, there were certain differences among the members. Mary, it seems, was the most heavenly minded of the three. She, after all, was the one who sat at the feet of Christ and anointed His feet with costly perfume, even wiping them dry with her hair. She hung on the Lord's every word, weighing all the things He said.

Martha had her own way of trying to please her Lord. Making the house tidy, scurrying to get things in order, running to do the shopping, racing to prepare the meals. And although she was distracted and anxious by all her busy serving, she probably assumed this was the best course of action.

Yes, the family members had their differences. Lazarus may have had serious physical problems. Martha was gently chided by the Lord for allowing the details of home-making and hospitality to divert her from fellowship with Him. Meditative Mary, on the other hand, received the Lord's commendation. She, said Jesus, had chosen what was better.

Yet John 11:5 tells us that Jesus loved them all.

That's good news. Not only to those who are strong, but also to the weaker members of the family of faith.

Perhaps you fall into the latter group.

"Me? I'm no great saint. I have a hard time getting into the Bible. I can't pray out loud. I don't seem to understand spiritual things the way others do. And sometimes I wonder if Jesus really cares for me as much He does for those who have it all put together."

If you see yourself like that, as a Martha perhaps, take heart. For just as a mother loves all of her children, even the weak and less gifted, so Christ cares for those who are weak in the faith...who wrestle with heavy burdens and temptations...who struggle with nagging doubts and fears.

If, on the other hand, you're one of the Marys, a real pillar of faith, please remember the counsel of Romans 14:1 to "accept him whose faith is weak."

So many of us don't. We're quick to judge and criticize those who are groping or slipping and can't seem to make the pieces fit. Few of us are willing to humble ourselves to help those who are weak in faith.

Whichever you are, and however you fit into the family—strong or weak—please know that Jesus loves you. He's reserved a special spot at His feet with your name on it.

He's ready for a closer relationship...whenever you are.

STRONGHOLD

For an inside look into Mary and Martha, find time today to read Luke 10:38-42 and John 11:17-44. Notice how differently these sisters react. How do you see yourself responding?

MY FATHER'S CREATION

If anyone is in Christ, he is a new creation.
2 CORINTHIANS 5:17

When we go camping with my parents, my elderly father is a wonder to watch. While others busy themselves with tents and stoves, ice chests and lanterns, he's out quietly gathering chunks of wood.

He'll come back to the campsite with an armload—trunks of gnarled redwood, juniper, or perhaps some pine that's had time to harden in the weather. Piling this trove near a comfortable rock, he sits down, pulls out his knives and begins whittling away the crusty bark and dead, dry, twigs. He scrapes off the dirt and any soft or decayed wood in the cracks of the stumps.

Some of the pieces he selects look utterly unredeemable. Yet he works on with deliberation, obviously with something very special in mind. Before you know it, a lovely piece of carved wood rests in his grip, shiny from the oil on his hands and smooth from the cut of his knife. The heart of that wood reveals a beautiful grain when the bark is chipped away. These lovely pieces are then fashioned into lamps, tables, chests, or stools.

Once while watching Daddy at his work, I did some work of my own—a charcoal sketch of him toiling away with his knife, cutting into a piece of wood. I entitled the rendering, "My Father's Creation."

I wanted to parallel the charcoal drawing with the idea

that our heavenly Father is hard at work in each of His children, creating something beautiful in us with the knife of His Word. The Holy Spirit peels away the crusty, dead layers of our old nature. He cuts out the decayed areas of habitual sin and lops off the dead or dying branches that don't produce fruit. Slicing away the diseased and damaged layers, His work reveals a changed heart, beautifully transformed by His sharp Word and His skilled hands.

"If anyone is in Christ," writes Paul, "he is a new creation; the old has gone, the new has come!... For we are God's workmanship, created in Christ Jesus to do good works" (2 Corinthians 5:17, Ephesians 2:10, NIV).

God in His Word can do that. Yes, the cut of the knife will be sharp, often painful. In our foolishness and fear we will want to cling to some of those dead, fruitless branches. But God works on with deliberation, obviously with something very special in mind—Christ Jesus in you.

STRONGHOLD

Just think—in Christ you are a brand new person on the inside. Turn to Romans 6 and look particularly at verses 1-11. What does it mean to consider yourself dead to sin but alive to God? Colossians 2:8-14 offers some exciting insight as well.

GRACE ON DISPLAY

The life of Jesus also may be manifested in our body.

2 CORINTHIANS 4:10

T he jade was exquisite. Smooth, glossy, and finely carved. Delicate gold chains cradled the light and returned it, ripe and mellow. Translucent opals graced their settings with milky fire.

Yes, I confess. I've been window shopping in the mall. I was only going to linger at the jewelry store window a moment, but the artistry of those precious stones held me a bit longer than I'd intended.

The diamonds, set against a black yard of velvet, were radiant—breaking the light into flashes of color. The contrast between the black velvet and the diamonds made those gems all the more brilliant. No other color cloth would have done—no blues, no grays, no pinks. Midnight velvet produced the best contrast.

It struck me as just one more illustration of how God works in our lives. It seems God best displays the brilliance of His grace against the backdrop of our dark and even blackest moments. Somehow, His grace is made all the more glorious when people see it at work in the lives of those who suffer.

Paul expressed a thought like that in a letter to the church in Corinth. "For God, who said, 'Let light shine out of darkness,' made his light shine in our hearts...We have this treasure [that is, the brilliance of God's grace] in jars of clay to show that this all-surpassing power is from God and not from us" (2 Corinthians 4:6a, 7, NIV).

As you read these words, you may feel as though your life is blanketed by blackness. Maybe you don't see much rhyme or reason behind that dark curtain of discouragement or grief right now. As difficult as this thought may be to understand, God may want to use your life as a display case for a time. He wants your life to be a setting where He can display His grace for all to see.

The contrast between your suffering and God's grace is going to catch people's eyes—believe me. Your life will be set apart from the rest of the ordinary stones and settings around you. Believers and unbelievers alike will be drawn to you. To observe the dark backdrop? No, not at all. But rather to wonder at the beauty and radiance of God's grace in your life.

You will discover that God's power shows up best against your weakness.

STRONGHOLD

The Bible talks about contrasts in 2 Corinthians 4:7-18. Ponder Paul's words and then consider this: The supremely valuable message of salvation has been entrusted by God to you, a frail and fallible human being. How does your life show up best the light and power of Christ within you?

MIND GAMES

*Rejoice with me, for I have found my sheep
which was lost!*

LUKE 15:6

I've got a problem with my prayer life. Perhaps you can identify with it. Let's say I've been dis-obedient…maybe lax in reading the Word, grumpy with Ken, or feeling just plain lousy, dull, and dried out. I know that prayer is a big part of the answer. So I begin to talk with God. But no sooner do I begin to pray than my mind starts playing games.

"Father, You are so full of mercy, so good. I agree with You that what I told that person was a half-truth—no, a lie. Thank You for forgiving me. I'm glad that's all behind me now, and I can go on.…" *Oh, come on now. God wants to see a little bit of repentance before He helps you out of this mess.*

"Well, uh…I know You are faithful and just to forgive me of my sins.…" *Yes, but you're not feeling sorry enough. Are you?*

"But I am. I truly am sorry for my sin." *Well, let's see a little bit more emotional involvement then! How long has it been since you've shed some tears? How much do you REALLY care?*

"I care. I care! God, You told me to acknowledge my sins, and I've done that. I confess I may not be in tears over that lie, but—" *Oh what's the use! God is probably so sick and tired of you piddling around with your Christian*

133

walk that He's probably hidden Himself from you anyway. If that's all the remorse you can drum up, just forget it!

Does that sound vaguely familiar? You know as well as I that if you wrestle with those mind games long enough, you'll throw in the towel and quit praying.

When that happens, I do my best to remember two important verses out of the book of Isaiah. Perhaps you'd do well to remember them also. Isaiah 30:18 is a favorite. That God can be the God of justice and at the same time long to show graciousness and compassion is a wonderfully comforting thought. Isaiah 45:19 is the other verse I look at.. When we truly desire mercy, God is ready to be found. There need be no cat-and-mouse mind games when we approach Him in prayer.

If we seek Him, He promises it won't be in vain. If we desire grace, He longs to give it to us. If we want comfort, He rises to show compassion.

As you pray today, remember those unchangeable truths about our Lord. Push aside the mind games and push through to Him, our God of compassion and love.

STRONGHOLD

"We can perhaps understand a God who would forgive sinners who crawl to Him for mercy," says Ken Taylor, "but a God who searches for sinners and then forgives them must have extraordinary love!" If you feel far from God, take comfort by reading Luke 15:3-10. God is searching for you!

HIS FINISHING TOUCH

*He who began a good work in you will carry it on
to completion until the day of Christ Jesus.*

PHILIPPIANS 1:6, NIV

I t was my first recording session. I had studied
for days, memorizing all the melodies. But what
really excited me was the thought of hearing it
all put together—violins, piano, horns, and harps.

To get an idea of how it was done, I went down to the
recording studio several days in advance, just to listen to
the musicians lay down the orchestral background music.
They gathered in a little studio, some of the top profes-
sionals in the country. The arranger put the score sheets
before them, and—believe it or not—after one rehearsal
they were ready for a take, and the sound they created was
breathtaking. Absolutely beautiful.

But do you know what happened after they got it
down on tape? Many of them left their seats and went on
break, milling around the rooms of the recording studio,
sipping on Cokes or coffee. They seemed totally detached
from the beauty of the music they had just had a part in
creating. Only one or two bothered to listen to the playback.

I couldn't believe it! How could these people create
something so extraordinary and then…just walk away
from it, not wanting to hear its final form?

Since that experience, I've thought about God's joy in
creating something beautiful in us. Philippians 1:6 tells us

that He will develop that good work that He has begun in our hearts and lives. He will perfect it and bring it to a full and satisfying completion.

You see, God doesn't walk away from His creation. He's not off somewhere relaxing between jobs, sipping on some refreshments. He's never nonchalant or aloof about the work of His hands. He's creating something beautiful in us—far more beautiful than a symphony.

For Him it's not simply another job that needs to be done. His reputation is at stake and His Son's image is the model. It's perfection that God has in mind—maturity in Christ, that's the end result.

God is always finding new ways of refining you and changing you and improving upon the score He's written with you in mind. He's at work in your life today, blending and sorting, and He's going to be there for the finishing touches. On the day of Jesus Christ, He'll be there with you for the playback.

All of heaven will be stunned to see and hear what His marvelous work has created in your life.

STRONGHOLD

God has you in mind as He composes the entire score of His kingdom. Want to hear what it's going to sound like? Turn to Revelation 5:11-14 and imagine yourself joining in the chorus of millions of angels.

A FRIEND

*But I have called you friends, for all things that I have
heard from My Father I have made known to you.*

JOHN 15:15

You've had it happen. You'll be going through a
heartache or a period of loneliness and you'll
want to tell a friend. Your phone call to share
your hurt, however, is persistently interrupted—or never
returned. Or worse, you draw a friend aside to describe
some of the things you've been going through and you get
the distinct impression your friend is distracted, only half
listening. You get little eye contact and a few, vague,
mumbled words for a reply.

Jesus had the same thing happen to Him. In Matthew
20:17-28, He and His disciples were on the road to
Jerusalem. It would be His last earthly journey. He knew
full well what awaited Him at the end of the road. He
poured out His heart to them, telling them exactly what
was going to happen when He passed through those city
gates.

Talk about unkind ears! The disciples not only ignored
His troubled words, they turned right around and began
arguing about who was going to be tops in the coming
kingdom, who was going to get the head honcho job or
the hotshot seat near the throne. Two of them even sent
their mother over to Jesus to argue their case. Unbelievable!

It breaks my heart to think of those unsympathetic disciples in Matthew 20 turning a deaf ear to Jesus at His

deepest point of need. If I had been there, I would like to think I would have held my Lord's hand, looked straight into His eyes, and said, "Please...tell me all about it." That's what friends are for.

Thankfully, Jesus understands. He knows what it feels like to have friends who can't, or perhaps don't always care. So He's the one who lends the sympathetic ear. His eye contact never falters. He will not be distracted from your cry. His heart is with yours in the middle of your pain.

"There is a friend," Scripture says, "who sticks closer than a brother" (Proverbs 18:24).

I've never had a brother, but I have the Friend. His name is Jesus. He listens and He cares.

STRONGHOLD

Do I—do you—really treat the Lord as a treasured friend? Think of all the special things friends share—heart-to-heart talks, the sacrifice of time, wants and needs, joys and sorrows, love and companionship. Jesus covers His side of friendship with you in John 15:15. As you read those words, and then read through that whole chapter, ask yourself, "How can I be a better friend to Jesus?"

YOU'RE NOT ALONE

We must do the work of him who sent me.

JOHN 9:4, NIV

Ever feel like you're the only one holding it all together?

If you didn't make that call or write that note, who would? The co-chairman of your committee is more than content to bask in the glory—and leave all the work to you. The dog would starve if you didn't feed it. The kitchen trash would overflow into the dining room unless you prodded and pleaded. You strongly suspect that the whole house (or church, or office, or Bible study, or carpool) would fall apart were it not for you, holding together all those loose ends by your fingers and toes.

You're not alone. In fact, you've got Somebody on your side who's taking more than His fair share of the load.

Look for a moment in the ninth chapter of John. Jesus is having a conversation with not only His disciples but also a man who had been blind from birth. "We must do the work of Him who sent Me." Whom was Jesus talking to in verse 4? I can't be sure, but I have a strong feeling He was looking directly at that disabled man.

I choose to think Jesus was reminding that blind man that he was not alone. He was not alone in his disability. He was not alone in his despair. The works of God were about to be displayed through him. The Lord wanted this man to know that God Himself was standing by his side, taking on more than His fair share of the load.

Jesus went on to actually heal the man, of course, but I think the Lord's words alone must have thrilled him beyond telling. Jesus was siding up with him to do the work of God. He was choosing him, saying, "We, my friend, must do the works of God. Together."

It awes me to think that Jesus wants me to help Him get the work of God done.

I'm not in it alone.

I don't have to weaken under the pressure.

It doesn't all fall on my sagging shoulders.

Christ stands with me—just as He stood with the blind man that day. And He's standing with you today, too. Especially if you feel you're desperately holding together all the loose ends. It won't all fall apart without you. Jesus is saying to you, "We—WE must do the works of God."

Jesus and you. Together. You couldn't be on a better team.

STRONGHOLD

If you want an idea of how the Lord takes on His fair share of your load, read Matthew 11:25-30. Jesus had in mind a double-yoke, two oxen sharing the weight of the same burden. As you "plow" through a heavy, frustrating schedule yoked with Jesus Christ, which one of you will take most of the weight? From where does the "rest" come?

ENLIGHTENED...BUT NOT LIT

*Be...imitators of those who through faith and patience
inherit the promises.*

HEBREWS 6:12

I'm sure you know people who have edged awfully close to the kingdom. In fact, you may have thought for sure they were Christians. They knew the right language, the right songs, the right tone of voice, the right facial expressions. They could recite the Four Spiritual Laws, pray with passion, and maybe even tell others about the Lord Jesus.

But then, mysteriously, they simply dropped out of sight. Poof. Spiritually speaking, they're no longer among us. If you asked them whether their commitment was real, they would just shrug their shoulders and say they really don't care.

I knew someone like that in high school. We went to the same Young Life weekend camp and even made a profession of faith in Christ on the same night. He wrote in my Bible and I wrote in his. We prayed together and talked about trusting and obeying.

But somewhere along the line, the light went out. As I think back on that young man, the words of Hebrews 6 come to mind. The writer speaks of those who have been "enlightened," who go so far as to "taste the heavenly gift," share in the Holy Spirit, and taste "the goodness of the word of God"—and then fall away!

It's a mystery to me—and a scary one at that—how a

person could be so close to Jesus Christ, so close to heaven, and then turn his or her back and walk away.

You could compare it to almost—but not quite—lighting a candle. If you hold a match near the wick of a candle, the candle itself almost glows. The wax has a luster. It shines. And all around the wick there's a kind of halo of illumination. You could say, in fact, that the candle is enlightened.

But it's not lit. The flame, though very close, has not ignited the wick. And there's quite a wide gap between being "enlightened" and actually being lit by the Spirit of God. A gap as wide as heaven and hell.

When someone slips away, does it make you question the security of your own salvation? Please don't let it. People who are genuinely enlightened exhibit all the evidences of close contact with the Spirit of God. But close only counts in horseshoes and hand grenades. It does not count when it comes to having one's name written in the Lamb's Book of Life.

Only Christians are lit. And once ignited, nothing in all the universe can put out that flame.

STRONGHOLD

Do you have the assurance that you are "lit," and not simply "enlightened"? Take a look at 2 Peter 1:5-11 and rejoice in the fact that you will one day receive a rich welcome into the eternal kingdom!

TRUTHS ONCE DESPISED

Blessed is the man whom God corrects.
JOB 5:17, NIV

The blind man had come to the one called Jesus for healing. And what did He do?

Jesus spit on the man's eyes.

To me, that's one of the most curious things Christ ever did in touching the life of a disabled person. Mark, chapter 8, records the whole incident for us. The healing isn't the curious part. After all, the Lord Jesus performed many such miracles. What's curious is the *way* in which He performed this particular miracle. The Lord spit in the man's eye!

Now you and I naturally associate a man's spit with...well, despicable things. Spit, we would all agree, is rather disgusting...even humiliating...especially when somebody else's spit ends up on you. Not to mention on your eyes!

But this was no ordinary man's saliva. And perhaps in employing this strange method of healing, Christ had teaching on His mind. Consider this thought. *It is possible that God will bless you by the very truth you once despised.*

Let me explain. When I was first injured and in the hospital, a well-meaning Christian friend stood by my bed and said, "Remember, Joni, God is sovereign. God is in control."

It felt as though that friend had just spit in my eye. I

was disgusted with the idea that God was in control. I despised a doctrine that told me God *could* have prevented my injury, but chose not to. How unthinkable.

In time, however, I was to discover the healing influence of that marvelous doctrine. As the months and years went by, I was able to praise God that He was in control. That there were no accidents in my life. That all things were fitting together for good. That He had reasons—and good ones—yet to be revealed.

Do you feel today as though God has spit in your eye? Do you feel betrayed, disgusted, and perhaps even tempted to despise your Lord for allowing such awful things to come into your life? Remember, it could be your very cure…as hard as that may be to believe or even stomach right now.

Give Him time. Circumstances may make no sense to you now. But if He has touched your life once, He will touch you again.

The spit from His mouth may be the means of opening your eyes.

STRONGHOLD

Do you feel confused, even betrayed, by some sad circumstances in your life? Read Job 5:17, Hosea 6:1, and Psalm 119:71. At first glance, the three verses will seem hard to fathom, but allow God to minister each as a healing balm to help soothe away the confusion and sense of betrayal. See the lasting results of God's justice in Job 5:17-27.

WHEN GOD STOOD STILL

And Jesus stopped and said, 'Call him here.'

MARK 10:49

e felt the excitement before he heard the sound. "Jesus of Nazareth is coming this way." He started yelling. "JESUS! Son of David! Have mercy on me!"

A cuff came out of the darkness. "Hush, you fool!"

The Nazarene stood still and ordered the man to be brought to Him. When he came near, Jesus asked him, "What do you want me to do for you?"

I've always loved that portion of Mark, chapter ten. There have been many times when I've felt just like Bartimaeus, the blind beggar at the gates of Jericho. Somehow I've aimlessly wandered off the path God has put me on. I've sinned—maybe deliberately, perhaps thoughtlessly. And I feel so far from God. I picture myself lost in a crowd, pushed to the side of the road, groping in the dark. I want to find my way back to the right path but sometimes feel too ashamed or discouraged even to approach God in prayer. I foolishly imagine God is busy somewhere else, tending to the prayers of other people who are more sincere, more valuable to the kingdom.

When things get that way, I picture poor Bartimaeus—lost and going nowhere. And sometimes I feel like whispering the same words. "Jesus, Son of David, have mercy on me." And somehow the hustle and bustle of the crowd stops. The Lord hears the call.

I love those two little words that describe the action Jesus took: "And Jesus stood still" (Mark 10:49, KJV). The Lord actually stopped what He was doing. The God of the universe stood still and beckoned the poor beggar to be brought to Him...simply because he asked for mercy.

I've wondered why the Lord was so moved with this one man. Surely there were other beggars in the crowd, just as lost. But this man had cried out from his heart. He wanted mercy. And sincerely believed that Jesus could deliver him.

That's what I need to remember when I've wandered away from the path God has put me on. Hebrews 4:16 says that when we approach the throne of grace with confidence, we do so that first we may receive *mercy*. Only after that will we find grace to help us in our time of trouble.

We needn't fear that Jesus is busy elsewhere in His vast universe. Or tending to the prayers of the "supersaints." Right now if you sense a deep spiritual need, if you feel the weight of guilt or regret crushing your shoulders, remember that Jesus of Nazareth is passing by.

Call out for mercy. And for you, God will stand still.

STRONGHOLD

For another story of God's mercy, read Matthew 9:9-13 and ask yourself: How has God shown unexpected kindness to me this week? How can I show mercy to one of my "enemies" today?

GOD'S BEST SECRET

My grace is sufficient for you.
2 CORINTHIANS 12:9

T he dictionary defines "secret" as something beyond normal comprehension...something obscure, hidden from view, concealed from knowledge. In light of that, it's curious that Paul says he has learned the "secret" of being content in any and every situation (Philippians 4:11-12).

Have you ever wondered what "secret" Paul was talking about?

The New Testament word translated "contentment" in our English Bibles means "sufficiency." I've been told that Paul uses the same Greek root here in Philippians that he does in 2 Corinthians 12:9, where he says God's grace is sufficient.

Perhaps Paul's secret of learning to be content was *simply learning to lean on God's grace.*

What a secret, this working of grace in our lives! Beyond our normal comprehension. Hidden from our view. Hard to explain. Impossible to pinpoint. Difficult to understand.

A friend of mine named Susan recently experienced unbearable pain with the sudden, unexpected breakup of her marriage. Even after a year, she's still picking up the pieces, the few fragments her husband left her when he broke their marriage vows for another woman. I watched

Susan go through months of agony, struggling against rejection and just plain nausea. But God's grace sustained her in a startling way. In fact, she commented to me just the other day that she believed the hardest thing to explain was how grace was at work in her life. To her, and to those of us who watched the tragedy, the sustaining, preserving, uplifting power of God's grace was truly a mystery. A wondrous secret none of us could understand.

All we could say was that God's grace was working. It was sufficient. For Susan, Jesus was enough.

Paul learned the secret of contentment. Susan is still learning the secret. How about you? Are you struggling today with discontentment, frustration, disappointment, or downright irritation? Take a moment to quiet your heart and listen to God's best secret...it's called grace, and it sounds like this:

Have hope. Take hold. He is sufficient.

STRONGHOLD

To learn some more secrets about grace, read Ephesians 2:8-9; Titus 2:11; 1 Peter 5:5; and Hebrews 12:15. Whom is grace for? What does God require of us to receive grace? What is the one drawback?

WHO HURTS THE MOST?

The Lord…was filled with pain.
GENESIS 6:6, NIV

A father warns his child time and again to stay away from all those bottles and containers underneath the sink. But one day it happens. Dad walks into the kitchen and sees his little boy, pale and unconscious, on the floor. Somehow the boy managed to pry the lid off that old bottle of insecticide and…

The paramedics arrive and, after a few anxious moments, revive the child. Yet in the coming days, the tragedy continues to unfold. Doctors report that the little boy will be permanently impaired with a mental handicap.

Although the boy has no concept of what life could have been if he had not disobeyed, his father will carry the pain of his son's disobedience for the rest of his life. It is he who must bear the hurt of awareness.

Let's apply this story to our relationship with God. Just who felt the deepest hurt back in the Garden of Eden? Adam and Eve? Yes, they must have suffered dreadfully as they began to live out the consequences of their disobedience. But how could they begin to reckon with the fact that their sons and daughters—throughout the long ages—would never, could never, be the same? They didn't begin to understand.

We can't understand either. Blinded by our fallen

nature, we have only the vaguest notion of what consequences our disobedience and sinful choices are causing in
our life and the lives of others.

But how about God the Father? He has complete
understanding. He can see not only what is and will be,
but also *what might have been.* He knows the full impact
of our permanent impairment by sin.

And does He grieve? Does the God of the universe sorrow over our sin and its terrible effects? Scripture indicates
that He feels anguish deeper than you and I could ever
understand.

But there is a piercing shaft of hope in these dark
reflections. A miracle drug has been applied. Christ's
blood on the cross is an antidote for the awful impairment
of sin. Though we can never flee from the consequences
of our sin, we can be restored. We can, in a sense, get back
into the Garden. Scripture tells us that "if we walk in the
light as He Himself is in the light, we have fellowship with
one another, and the blood of Jesus His Son cleanses us
from all sin" (1 John 1 :7).

We who have brought such grief to the heart of God
can also bring joy and delight and companionship as we
accept His cure and walk with His Son.

STRONGHOLD

*To better understand how we grieve God, read Genesis 6:5-6;
Judges 10:16; Hosea 11:8; Luke 19:41-42; 13:34; and
Ephesians 4:30. Then in prayer, ask God to forgive you and
to apply His healing balm—His love and grace.*

Gen 6:6 His heart was filled w/ pain.
Jud. 10:6 He felt sorry for them when He saw their pain.
Luke 19:41 Jesus cried for the city of Jerusalem

"LIFE WOULD BE GREAT IF ONLY..."

The Lord is my shepherd, I shall not want.

PSALM 23:1

What do quadriplegics daydream about? Running a marathon? Ballroom dancing? Climbing a mountain? Not necessarily. Many of us have scaled down our fantasies.

Life would be great if only I were a paraplegic...then I could use my hands.

I can't tell you how many times I've thought that. Times when I'm feeling sorry for myself. Times when I'm battling a big inferiority complex. I see these paraplegics who can transfer themselves out of their wheelchair into their own bed, reach for things in the refrigerator, wash dishes at a sink, quickly sort through the mail...and the old feelings of hurt and despair start to slink back into my heart.

Disabled people who have use of their hands have it easy. Yes, I actually think thoughts like that when my self-image is at a low.

But I don't think I'm alone. Even able-bodied people make the mistake. We look at others who seem more attractive, smarter, richer, healthier. People who seem to get all the "breaks" in life. Then, when we look back at ourselves, our minor defects begin to look like deformities.

Fortunately, the Bible has good advice for us when we get down on ourselves. In Colossians 2:10, Paul tells us that we have been given "fullness in Christ." In other words, we are COMPLETE in Him. Peter agrees. The apostle writes, "His divine power has given us everything we need for life and godliness" (2 Peter 1:3, NIV).

Once we comprehend this amazing truth, our minor—or major—defects become reminders of how complete we really are in Christ. The inferiority complex begins to release its grip. And I'm content.

To stay that way, I weave the contents of 2 Corinthians 12:9 through the fabric of my spirit: "But he said to me, 'My grace is sufficient for you, for my power is made perfect in weakness.' Therefore I will boast all the more gladly about my weaknesses, so that Christ's power may rest on me" (NIV).

One of these days it's going to sink into my thick skull that *I wouldn't be happier* if I were a para rather than a quad. I am complete in Him. The fullness of Christ dwells within me. Because of that, I am lacking nothing. In fact, I have everything to gain. The power of Christ rests upon me because of my infirmities. Therefore, I will gladly boast as a quad.

You can't improve on "complete."

STRONGHOLD

Is there anything you honestly lack? If there's a shade of doubt, turn to Psalm 23 and zero in on the very first verse. Think of at least five ways of saying, "The Lord is my shepherd, I shall lack nothing."

RESPONDING TO YOUR ACCUSERS

*Let all be harmonious, sympathetic, brotherly,
kindhearted, and humble in spirit.*

1 PETER 3:8

I magine you're being set up. Framed. And you know it. You're about to be accused of some terrible wrong you had nothing to do with. Trumped-up charges are bouncing around at your office. Malicious gossip circulates wherever you go. Whispers and nudges and cold shoulders.

What would you say to the people who connived those awful things?

Or, let's say you're about to face your boss because of such charges. Your enemies have spread more lies and swayed the opinions of even your best friends. People turn the other way in the lunch room. You've been deserted and you're left alone to make your own defense.

What words would you have? Not only for your accusers but your friends? How would you feel? What would you do?

Jesus found himself in that exact predicament. The night He was having an intimate dinner with His disciples was the very night the plot to betray Him was revealed. He knew His accuser was right in the middle of the fellowship. He also knew that at that very moment His critics were trumping up charges against Him. He knew people would say all sorts of false, slanderous things against Him. He even knew that His dearest friends, Peter and John, would abandon Him like some sort of leper that very night.

What could He say at such a moment? What would He do?

John 13:4 says He got up from the meal, took off His outer clothing, wrapped a towel around His waist…and began to wash His disciples' feet, even those of Judas.

What would you have done if you were the Lord? I probably would have grabbed Judas by the scruff of the neck and said, "See here, jerk, I'm up to your evil tricks. There's no way you're going to get away with this." Then I would have punched him in the jaw.

What did Jesus do? He washed the man's feet.

Christ even goes on in that same chapter to remind us, "I have set you an example that you should do as I have done for you.… Now that you know these things, you will be blessed if you do them" (vv. 15, 17 NIV).

Scripture is clear. In the face of unfairness and betrayal, you are to be humble, not angry. And whatever He asks you to do, He will empower you to do.

May God give you grace to respond in humility, like Jesus.

STRONGHOLD

Jesus set us an example to follow in 1 Peter 2:18-25. So how do we follow an example like that? The advice is to the point in 1 Peter 3:8-12.

COMING ATTRACTIONS

Teach us to number our days.

PSALM 90:12

Long ago and far away, on a wintry night on the farm, my sister and I bundled up and stepped outside to gaze at the beautiful nighttime sky. It was one of those nights when the air is sparkling clear and the sky is ablaze with God's light and glory.

I remember that particular night so well because Jay and I started talking about heaven. As we stood together, our breath making little clouds in the night air, one of us reminded the other of James 4:14: "What is your life? You are a mist that appears for a little while and then vanishes" (NIV).

Trouble is, you and I don't think of life down here on earth lasting "a little while." Until circumstances confront us with reminders of our own mortality, we tend to think and act as if this life will go on forever.

But it won't.

This life is not going to go on forever—nor is it the best life we will experience. The good things down here on earth are merely images of the better things we'll know one day in heaven.

It's like my paintings. I like to go out into the country-side to paint and sketch landscape scenes, examples of God's creation. Using the best techniques I know, I seek to imitate the panorama before me. But those drawings are, at best, only a feeble, sketchy attempt to mirror what I see. With the limited capacity of brushes and acrylics, I approximate what God has painted in an infinite array of colors. My works will always be bounded by the edges of the canvas. They can never fully portray God's limitless handiwork above and beneath and around me.

This earth that we know is a rough sketch—a kind of preliminary rendering—of the glory that will one day be revealed.

It's like stealing a tiny sip of stew before dinner. You haven't had a meal, but you have had a little foretaste of what to expect when you get to the table. The happiest, most joyous moments of your life are God's way of whetting your appetite for even greater joys, greater fulfillment to come.

So let's not get too settled in, too satisfied with the fine things down here on earth. They're only previews of the coming attractions.

The main feature is only moments away.

STRONGHOLD

Read Psalm 90 and gain a bit of the perspective Moses had on life. In view of the brevity of life, what was Moses' prayer in verse 12? Ask the Lord to grant you His perspective on time and life as you seek to make the most of today's opportunities.

MORE THAN MEETS THE EYE

Behold, the fear of the Lord, that is wisdom.

JOB 28:28

The physics teacher was explaining to his twelfth grade class how orderly and full of design the universe is. To illustrate his point, he gave a demonstration that at least one girl in the class would never forget. The girl was me.

First he took a flat piece of metal—and sprinkled salt across its surface. The sheet was welded to a metal rod, which he held like an umbrella. Holding the rod, he raised the sheet and we all crowded around to see what he might do next.

He took a violin bow and gently stroked the edge of the metal. A note of music resounded throughout the classroom. But something else was happening on top of the vibrating metal sheet. Incredibly, the salt crystals began to arrange themselves into little patterns. Tiny quadrangles!

He stroked the bow at a different angle and new patterns formed—perfect little hexagons—as the crystals responded to the music.

We all stood around with our mouths open. Our teacher smiled, not even needing to add to the lesson from nature. Even music had a kind of mathematical design and visible order that we had never even thought of—or dreamed of. Which reminds me of the words of

Paul to the Corinthians: "No eye has seen, no ear has heard, no mind has conceived what God has prepared for those who love him" (1 Corinthians 2:9, NIV).

That little example was something my eyes did see and my ears did hear—and it will remain in my heart for a long time to come. Can you think how incredible, though, it's going to be when we meet Jesus and get to see and hear and know things that we can't even dream of here on earth? Spiritual things, yes, but also knowledge about the order and design of this universe—physics and music and geometry—things Einstein never considered in his wildest imagination.

God has prepared all this and much, much more for those who love Him. Here and now, these thoughts remind me how deeply I need to lean on the wisdom and counsel of the Holy Spirit as I move through the "mundane" activities of my day. Each day of living has eternal dimensions we can't begin to imagine in our limited minds.

There is more to life than meets the eye—or ear!

STRONGHOLD

For those who belong to the heavenly Father, scientific demonstrations can refresh a sense of awe and wonder within us. These are not simply "patterns of nature," they are the designs of a master Designer! Read Job 28:20-28. What does Job say about wisdom in the creation around us?

GRACE FOR TODAY...ONLY

*Therefore do not worry about tomorrow, for
tomorrow will worry about itself.
Each day has enough trouble of its own.*

MATTHEW 6:34, NIV

was sharing some thoughts recently with a group
of prisoners at a maximum-security facility.
Gathered around me were seventy to eighty men
who had come to Christ in that prison. I was asked to
give them a few words of encouragement. As I looked
into the eyes of those brothers, I spoke about the sustaining grace of our Lord Jesus—how His power shows up
best in our weakness. The men all nodded and said their
"amens."

I asked several of them how much time they had yet to
serve. Some had only a few months, others many years.
Then I confessed something very personal. I told them,
rather hesitantly, how weak-kneed I sometimes get when I
think about living twenty, even thirty, more years in a
wheelchair. A number of the men nodded silently.
Looking down at my wheelchair, I told them I had my
own bolts and bars to live with.

No doubt, those prisoners get a little weak-kneed themselves, thinking about decades behind bars and barbed
wire. Even though they've accepted their circumstances, it's
tough to face a future of confinement and limitations.

Before I left them, I related a simple, yet very special
secret that helps me face the future with confidence. The

secret is simply this: God does not expect me to accept what may or may not happen to me twenty years from now.

God does not give me grace for those future uncertain years. He doesn't give me grace for next year's headaches—or even next month's heartaches. He won't even loan me enough grace to face the prospects of tomorrow! God only gives me grace for today. He expects me to live this day in His strength, leaning on His wisdom, drawing on His presence and power.

And that's what He expects of you today. To live one day at a time. To redeem each hour. To make the most of the moment. To live richly and abundantly by His grace. He doesn't expect you to handle the burden of next week or next month or next year. So whether you're in pain…in prison…in a hospital…in a difficult marriage…in a deteriorating financial situation or a devastating family crisis…wherever you are, by God's grace make the most of today. And leave the future to Him.

STRONGHOLD

Read Hebrews 4:16 and dissect the verse, asking the standard "five W's and an H" questions. To WHOM is the verse written? WHAT is promised? WHERE do we find grace? WHEN do we receive it? WHY was it given? And HOW do we ask?

SUNDAY MORNING HASSLES

*I will bless the LORD who has counseled me; Indeed, my
mind instructs me in the night.*

PSALM 16:7

I t's almost predictable. In the Sunday morning rush to get up, scarf down breakfast, gather notebooks and Bibles, and warm up the van, somebody's bound to get irritated. Ken and I aren't always quick to detect a problem, but when a frosty silence descends inside the van on a sunny California morning, it's obvious one of us has a problem.

Once we're in church, the irritation often melts away. We both apologize and affirm our love for each other. But then we get into trouble all over again if, on the way home, we try to pinpoint the source of the original irritation.

Recently while driving alone in the van I tuned in James Dobson's "Focus on the Family" broadcast. I was just in time to hear the good doctor interviewing a group of mothers about life at home on Sunday mornings. Now that grabbed my attention! To my surprise (and relief!) Dr. Dobson mentioned he and Shirley have had their worst arguments on the way to church on Sundays. He feels there is real satanic pressure put on believers on the Lord's day morning.

I got home, pulled into the driveway, and as Ken came out the kitchen door to meet me, I said, "Guess what! Jim Dobson says that Sundays are the pits for him and Shirley at times. Isn't that great news?"

A slow and surprised smile spread across Ken's face. "Really?" he said.

If the words *praise* and *worship* share anything in common, it is this: When we praise and worship God, we are doing the most unselfish thing we could possibly do. True praise and worship permit no self-centeredness. We must step outside of our own complaints, irritations, and desires, focusing instead on the greatness of God.

Perhaps that's why the devil makes the extra effort to entangle us in quarrels on Sunday mornings. He hates praise. He despises our worship of God. He will go to any length to thwart that purpose. And the Enemy succeeds when we allow self-centeredness to consume us, entangling us in our complaints rather than focusing on our Lord.

Well, Sunday's a-coming. Are you alert? Aware? Prepared? Let's not allow the Enemy to rob us of the privilege of worship.

STRONGHOLD

You can prevent those Sunday morning hassles. And it can begin on Saturday night. Read several psalms of praise and worship before retiring. God can work on your heart, mind, and emotions through the night—just take a look at Psalm 16:7.

"CAN'T SAY ENOUGH..."

And He is the radiance of His glory.

HEBREWS 1:3

W hen I was working on my third book, *Choices...Changes,* there was one episode I especially enjoyed writing. You guessed it. It was the last episode, about my husband.

It was great fun to sit at the computer with my friend and describe Ken Tada. How he looked the first time I saw him...how he talked...how he smiled...how he carried himself...how he moved when he played racquetball. The words about our dating days flowed effortlessly. Writing about our wedding day and marriage was pure joy. Obviously, I didn't need a thesaurus to think of adjectives. I wanted to go on and on.

I'll bet it's the same with those you love, too. You want others to know how special that person is—whether it's your mate, your friend, your child, your niece, your nephew, or your grandchild. The best part is finding someone genuinely interested in *listening* to your glowing descriptions. It actually multiplies your pleasure.

Listen to the author of Hebrews talk about his best Friend, Jesus, in Hebrews 1:1-4. It's as if someone had approached him and said, "You seem to put a great deal of stock in this Person, Jesus Christ. Just who is He, anyway? Why are you so excited about Him? Can you describe Him?"

Could he ever! Finding a listening ear, the writer can't say enough. Look at the seven descriptive phrases he uses in the first four verses of his book: "appointed heir of all things," "through whom he made the universe," "radiance of God's glory," "exact representation of his being," "sustaining all things by his powerful word," "provided purification for sins," "sat down at the right hand of the Majesty in heaven."

With the ink flowing fast on his parchment, the writer goes on and on. Chapter one, chapter two, chapter three, chapter four...Jesus, Jesus, Jesus, Jesus.

How is it with you? Are you looking for listening ears, anxious to go on and on about the Lord Jesus and what He means to you?

If you find you don't have enough adjectives to describe Him, I'd like to introduce you to the author of Hebrews. Maybe the two of you can get away together for a few minutes today.

There's nothing that excited writer would love more than a listening ear.

STRONGHOLD

This evening just before bed, take fifteen minutes to slowly meditate on the descriptions of Jesus given in these scriptures, thanking Him for who He is: Isaiah 53:3; Daniel 7:9; Matthew 12:18; Mark 1:24; Luke 1:78; John 3:2; 8:58; 1 Corinthians 10:4; 2 Corinthians 9:15; Ephesians 2:20; 1 Timothy 1:1; 2:5-6.

YOUR FIRST RESPONSE

Let your speech always be with grace.
COLOSSIANS 4:6

Typing always involves a team effort here at Joni and Friends. When Francie and I sit down at the computer, her fingers can barely keep up with my thoughts as they come. I talk, she types.

This morning we were really humming. The ideas flowed with ease. The right Scriptures were on the tip of my tongue. Phrases fell into place like puzzle pieces. It all came together. I was so delighted with the results I immediately asked Francie to print out a hard copy of our labors. Which button should she push, Francie wondered. *That* one, I assured her.

Then—in an instant—*ffzzzzt!* All of our morning's work blipped into the twilight zone. Gone! Irretrievable!

I bit my lip. I felt like complaining loudly and bitterly. But instead of committing myself to a bunch of words I might regret, I simply screamed. In fact, we both looked at each other and screamed!

I thought of that recently as I was reading in the book of Acts. Peter and John had been thrown into prison. Nothing unusual about that. Getting jailed became one of those everyday annoyances to the apostles. The next day they were hauled before Israel's religious and political hierarchy and were told that any further teaching in the name of Jesus would mean harsh repercussions.

What then, was the church's response when Peter and John returned to the fellowship and reported all these things? Acts 4:24 records the first comments out of their mouths: "Sovereign Lord," they said, "you made the heaven and the earth and the sea, and everything in them" (NIV).

"Sovereign Lord," we hear them say. Not "Oh no" or "Oh darn" or "I can't believe it" or "Why us?" Instead, we hear them exclaim the joy of their conviction—that God was in control, that there was a plan and a purpose and all they had to do was acknowledge that wonderful truth. In short, they worshiped.

In verse 28 they went on to acknowledge that the authorities had only done what God's "power and will had decided beforehand should happen." They ended their prayer with a plea for confidence and boldness to faithfully proclaim the message of Christ.

When you get up on the wrong side of the bed, choose the wrong route to work, or push the wrong button, be ready with a word of worship. *Sovereign Lord, do whatever You like. You are in control. Grant me the courage to bear up and speak Your name with confidence.*

STRONGHOLD

Take a look at Daniel 6:5-16 for a glimpse at a man whose first response always seemed to be the right response. Make an exchange! Trade any not-so-nice words and actions for words of thanks and actions of obedience.

WHATEVER HAPPENED TO PALM WEDNESDAY?

God save the Son of David! Blessed is the man who comes in the name of the Lord! God save him from on high.
MATTHEW 21:9, PHILLIPS

Shouting their joyful hosannas, the people shared their expectation of Jesus as the coming King. This was the one who would throw the Roman oppressor out of the Holy City. He would release them from the terrible burden of taxes. He would feed them, provide for and protect them, and give them national dignity once again.

But as the week wore on, the mood of the crowd changed. Why wasn't the Nazarene making His move? Sure, He continued to heal and teach in the temple. But He remained aloof and reclusive, retreating to a nearby village every night, spending time with His disciples outside the city walls. When was He going to *do* something? When was He going to take control? Why wasn't He spending time with the "right" people—the savvy political types who got things done?

Little wonder the mood of the people soured by midweek. "Maybe this Man's not all He's cracked up to be," they may have reasoned. "Maybe He's been pulling the wool over our eyes all this time. He's probably powerless to do any real good around here."

The rest is history. The crowds turned on Him and screamed for His crucifixion—not more than a week after

167

they had celebrated His entry into the city.

I wonder…are we all that different from those people?

When expectations are running high, when we think we've got God's plan neatly figured, when we've convinced ourselves that the King's job is to make our lives easier, relieve our burdens, and take away our everyday pressures…don't you think our praises may sound a bit empty?

What happens when the shouts of Palm Sunday fade into Blue Monday? What happens when we hit midweek and all our plans have splintered like a ship's hull on a reef? Can we still sing our hosannas? Or do we turn on God in bitterness or resentment because He didn't follow through on our list of expectations?

Let's be sure we give Jesus praise for who He is…not what we think He ought to be.

STRONGHOLD

Psalm 103 is a great psalm to use when you want to praise God for exactly who He is. Notice how the psalm begins and ends. Personalize verses 2-5. Ask God right now to help you praise Him from your innermost being.

LET DOWN YOUR NET

*Put out into the deep water and let down
your nets for a catch.*

LUKE 5:4

I
t was one of those dry times. The Bible seemed about as inspiring as the Los Angeles phone book. My prayers never seemed to make it more than two or three feet into the air. I would have been happy to get them as high as the ceiling.

My Christian friends kept going on and on about all they were learning and how they were growing and what God was telling them and *wasn't the Lord wonderful?* I felt little interest in spiritual things. Faking it made me feel even more guilty.

The hardest part was that I couldn't trace the dry spell to anything specific. No besetting sins. No fights with my husband. No roots of bitterness. No great lapses in my prayer life or Bible study. No lack of fellowship. Yet my spirit felt as arid as July in the Mojave Desert.

Strange as it sounds, the closest biblical analogy I can find for those dry days takes place in the middle of a lake. It is the story of Jesus asking Simon Peter to push out into deep water to cast his nets (see Luke 5:3-8).

Simon was weary. Tired of trying. His back ached and his eyelids drooped. He'd been at it all night long without so much as a sardine to show for it. Yet at the command of Christ, he let down his nets. One more time.

Perhaps all of your nets are empty today. You've tried

and tried but have come up with nothing. You feel dry and dull and wonder if God has misplaced your file somewhere on His desk.

He hasn't! God has been listening to your prayers. As a matter of fact, it's often those petitions offered in the dry times that please Him best.

Your heavy heart is no secret to the God who loves you. As David wrote: "All my longings lie open before you, O LORD; my sighing is not hidden from you" (Psalm 38:9, NIV).

He's asking you today to let down your net. One more time. Obey the word of Christ and let down your net. Keep in the Word. Return to prayer. Confess your sin. Get accountable to a Christian friend. Worship with God's people. Sooner or later, He'll surprise you just as He surprised Simon Peter. He's going to bring you out of that long night—out of that dryness. You're going to experience His joy...more than you can handle.

Be faithful. Trust Him. Wait. Jesus can still fill an empty net.

STRONGHOLD

The Spirit of Christ can revive us out of a dry spell. For a good word picture, read Isaiah 35:1-7. That portion of Scripture is talking about the return of the Lord Jesus, but the beautiful descriptions can also apply to you today.

IF YOU CAN GLORIFY GOD IN THIS...

*Man's chief end is to glorify God and to
enjoy Him forever.*

WESTMINSTER SHORTER CATECHISM

While dieting a few months ago, I turned down at a friend's house a luscious-looking piece of walnut cake topped with whipped cream icing and a sprinkling of nuts.

My friend regarded me for a moment. "If you can turn down *this,*" she said, "then you can turn down anything."

Maybe you've said something similar as a student taking way too many units for your own good—and working nights to boot. As the pressure builds, the midnight oil burns, and finals loom, you hear yourself say, "If I can make it through *this* semester, I can make it through anything!"

You can almost hear God say the same thing to us...as we wade through crushing disappointments...or battle a confusing family problem...or grit our teeth and learn contentment in the middle of a painful illness...or tearfully accept the sudden loss of a loved one.

We might at first think it curious that God so often uses suffering to make our lives "to the praise of His glory," as it says in Ephesians. I mean, aren't there better ways we can glorify God—or at least easier ones? But do you know what God says to us? "If you can praise and glorify Me in *this* circumstance, My child, you can glorify Me in anything."

In other words, whenever a Christian is found faithful in affliction, repaying good for evil, returning love for abuse, holding steadfast through suffering, or loving in the middle of loneliness or grief, the Lord receives the truest, brightest, most radiant kind of glory possible.

And if we can be found glorifying Him in that manner, God will open up all kinds of new opportunities, new circumstances in which to glorify Him. He'll do so because He knows we can be trusted, we can handle it with His grace.

If you can glorify God through a patient response right now—in the middle of those things—then you can glorify God anywhere.

Kind of puts you on the victory side doesn't it?

STRONGHOLD

Take a look at 1 Corinthians 10:31. Eating and drinking—very average, ordinary circumstances—remind us that all of our average, daily routines can be opportunities to give God glory. Think of five everyday responsibilities and decide how you can give God glory through each one.

REFLECTIONS IN THE FURNACE

I will bring [them] into the fire;
I will refine them like silver.
ZECHARIAH 13:9, NIV

The only things that caught fire were the ropes that bound their hands and feet.

The king, who had ordered the servants of God thrown into the fire for refusing to worship his golden image, stood as close as he dared to the mouth of the furnace and shouted to them. "'Shadrach, Meshach and Abednego, servants of the Most High God, come out! Come here!'

"So Shadrach, Meshach and Abednego came out of the fire.... The fire had not harmed their bodies, nor was a hair of their heads singed; their robes were not scorched, and there was no smell of fire on them" (Daniel 3:26, 27).

Not only were the three young men free from burns or injuries, they didn't even smell like smoke! And their God was blessed by the king (verses 28-30).

At one time or another, all of us have felt the flames of the refiner's fire. No matter how we balk at the idea, God has promised to refine His children.

To refine, says Webster, is "to make fine or pure; free from impurities, dross, alloy, or sediment...to free from imperfection, coarseness, crudeness, etc." A refiner's fire, of course, is supposed to improve whatever commodity goes into it. Look at your gold wedding band or maybe that gold chain around your neck. After all these years, it still wears well. It has the luster and richness pressed into it long ago when it went through the refining flames.

But how many of us go through the refiner's fire and come out the other end looking like...charcoal? Or rusty iron. Or smoking ashes. Often when we come through a period of suffering, we want to make sure that everybody knows all the sad and sordid details. The thing of beauty that God wanted to create by sending us into the flames becomes tarnished by our complaints and woebegone expressions.

Be honest. If you've had one of those days when you feel as if you've been dragged through the refiner's fire, how do you show it? By boasting about your trials? If you do, I'm afraid people are going to smell smoke. Your testimony may end up tarnished. Even scorched.

There's a better way. Let's offer sincere, wholehearted praise to God as we walk through the refiner's fire. Perhaps those who pause to peer into our furnace will see the Son of God walking with us, as he did with Shadrach, Meshach and Abednego.

STRONGHOLD

Take a look at 1 Peter 1:3-12. (Remember, Peter was writing to Christians who were facing lions in the coliseum.) According to Peter, exactly why does God permit trials to come our way?

THE SOUND OF A CRY

Give ear to my words, O LORD.

PSALM 5:1

nobody is as in touch, in tune, with our heart's longings as God.

In Psalm 5, David opens his prayer by saying, "Give ear to my words, O LORD, consider my groaning. Heed the sound of my cry." Up to his ears in trouble, his heart pounding in fear, David wants God to hear the *sound* of his cry.

Does that ring a bell with any of you mothers? Your baby is nestled in his crib upstairs and suddenly you hear him cry. After a moment of listening, you know what that child wants by simply interpreting the *sound* of his crying. You can tell whether he's just tired and grumpy—or if he's waking up and wants you to come running. You can tell if he's afraid, lonesome, or actually in pain. Mothers learn to heed—and read—the voice of crying. They know what their child wants simply by the sound of his voice.

God is like that. When we pray, He knows just what our need is even if we can't shape the words. He can tell if it's an urgent prayer for help, a sighing prayer of discouragement, or maybe just a deep-down groan that we only half understand ourselves. Much like a mother with a child, God heeds and pays special attention to the voice of our cry.

He also listens for our praise.

Just as that mom is deeply moved by the cry of her child, she is overjoyed with the sound of his laughter. A smile, a gurgle, and a squeal delight a mother. And as that child grows, it means even more to hear him say, "Mom, you're something special. You're the neatest mom on the whole block."

Wouldn't you think our praise to God would delight Him all the more? If God heeds the sound of our cry, it makes sense that He also delights in the sound of our praise.

What about taking time out today to go before your Lord? Invite Him to read your heart, those secret pages no one has ever turned. Let Him hear the voice of your cry, all of those deep, inexpressible fears and longings. It doesn't have to involve a lot of words or carefully constructed phrases. Your time with the Lord can just be a quiet pause in the day, perhaps even a time of silence. God knows that voice of yours. Just like a mother, He knows exactly what you need when you cry to Him.

STRONGHOLD

Recall the most meaningful times you've enjoyed with family. Now transfer some of those warm feelings to your relationship with your heavenly Father. Imagine His joy when He hears your praise. Think of how instant He is in responding to your cry. Talk with Him now—straight from the heart.

THE GROANING OF THE SPIRIT

The Spirit helps us in our weakness.
ROMANS 8:26, NIV

I mmediately after church, a young woman with cerebral palsy approached me in her wheelchair. This woman's speaking was especially difficult to grasp. She kept groaning a certain sentence over and over again. Even though I patiently asked her to repeat each word one by one, I still couldn't understand. The expression on her face gave me no clues at all.

Finally, after many attempts, I was able to piece her sentence together. She was asking me to help her find someone who could assist her into the restroom! It was a simple request. But I felt helpless, so inadequate, that it had taken me so long to understand her.

Can you imagine the hardship of not even being able to make your needs known? Wouldn't it be sad if there were no one around who could even understand you?

And yet that is the very predicament in which you and I find ourselves (Romans 8:26-27). There are times when we want to talk to God...but somehow can't manage it. The hurt goes too deep. Fear locks our thoughts. Confusion scatters our words. Depression grips our emotions.

I'm so glad God can read my heart and understand what's going on even when I am handicapped by my own weakness for words. As it says in Hebrews 4:13,

"Nothing…is hidden from God's sight. Everything is uncovered and laid bare before the eyes of him to whom we must give account."

When we are in such trouble that we can't even find words—when we can only look toward heaven and groan in our spirit—isn't it good to remember that God knows exactly what's happening? The faintest whisper in our hearts is known to God. Even if it should be a sigh so faint that you are not even aware of it yourself, He has heard it. And not only heard it, but He *understands* it—right down to the slightest quiver registered in our inner-most being.

You and I may certainly be handicapped when it comes to understanding the groans and sighs of one another. And others—even those closest to us—may never be able to hear or interpret our deepest sorrows and longings.

But the One who searches hearts knows and understands. The Spirit is never handicapped by our weakness for words.

Our heavenward groans have a voice before God.

STRONGHOLD

Aren't you glad the Holy Spirit wraps words around your feelings—especially when you don't seem to have words to pray? I'm sure Solomon would not mind loaning you his prayer recorded in 1 Kings 8:56-61. Personalize it and make it your prayer to God.

WHAT MAKES HEAVEN "HOME"?

And I saw a new heaven and a new earth.
REVELATION 21:1

R eading the descriptions of heaven and the New Jerusalem in the Bible gives us an incredible picture. All sorts of word pictures describe the beauty and majesty of that place...streets of translucent gold, gates made of precious stone, a throne from which flows a river, walls made of brightly colored gems.

When I think of heaven as a *home,* however, I hardly ever think about mansions or glittery streets. If heaven really is our long-awaited dwelling, what draws us to that place? For that matter, what makes any house a home? It's not necessarily its shape or size or furniture, is it? When we think of our earthly home, we don't usually think about the four walls. *What makes home is not what a place looks like, but who lives there.*

As far as I'm concerned, that's what makes heaven so appealing. It's no longer a bunch of word pictures describing rainbow thrones and twenty-four-karat asphalt. It's a place where *people* live—and wonderful people, at that. Friends of mine who have left this earth. Relatives who have long since gone to be with the Lord. Add to that the countless saints of the ages like Moses and David, Joshua and Daniel, Naomi and Ruth, Paul and Peter, and even saints in our own age—Amy Carmichael or Corrie Ten

Boom—people who have inspired my walk in the Lord. I can't wait to meet them.

On top of that long list of people is Jesus Christ Himself. And the Father. And the Holy Spirit.

Certainly, heaven is a prepared place. But more importantly, it's a place for prepared people. People who will not only enjoy fellowship with one another, but with our great Creator and Savior.

If you find it difficult to muster up longing for those celestial mansions and glimmering vistas, try taking your focus off heaven as a *place*. Put your focus on heaven as a home…a home for people like you, who love the Lord Jesus.

STRONGHOLD

Are you one of those "prepared people"? What proof could you give of your love and faithfulness if this life left you totally unscarred? How could you appreciate at all the scarred hands with which Christ will greet you? Get better prepared today by spending a few moments alone with Colossians 3:1-4.

PRAYING IN HIS NAME

My Father will give you whatever you ask in my name.
JOHN 16:23, NIV

Handicapped people are puzzled, and I can't say I blame them. One pastor tells them faith healing is theirs to "claim." Another insists divine healing is theirs only if God sees fit. Cassette sermons urge "emotional healing" and Christian magazine articles describe "spiritual healing." *No wonder* they're puzzled.

I had to see for myself, so I flicked on Sunday evening television last week. Sure enough, the clergyman at the microphone was expounding that God WANTS you well, so you CAN and SHOULD be well. I just wish that TV preacher could visit our office, sit quietly for a few hours, and read some of the letters we receive from disabled people who have viewed his program. After years of praying, these people have nearly had their faith shipwrecked by the "health-wealth" way of looking at their problems.

When I was first paralyzed, you can imagine how interested I was in what the Bible had to say about healing. I desperately wanted out of my wheelchair! As I pored over Scripture, I was impressed that Jesus never seemed to pass up anybody. He showed His concern for the suffering by opening the eyes of the blind and the ears of the deaf—and even raising up the paralyzed.

I was also struck with the number of Bible verses, especially John 16:23-24, that seemed to indicate I could ask whatever would be in God's will—and Jesus would do it. I put two and two together and figured if Jesus healed back then, He'd want to raise me up now. Why shouldn't healing a suffering teenaged girl be perfectly consistent with His will?

To make a long story very short, I never got healed. At least not the sort of healing I was after. It was years later that I began to catch a glimpse of all that a verse like John 16:23 might mean.

What does it mean to pray in Jesus' name? I've come to understand it means to pray in a manner consistent with Christ's character, or life. When we pray in Jesus' name, we should expect to receive qualities consistent with that name—with His character. Traits such as patience and self-control and assurance. We might pray for financial prosperity, a new career, success with the opposite sex, or physical healing, but God may choose to give us something even more precious, something even closer to what His name and character are all about. Joy. Joy that we might be complete…whatever our circumstances.

STRONGHOLD

Do you and I really appreciate the sweeping access we have to the Father? To get a clearer idea of what it means to go to God "in Jesus' name," take a close look at Hebrews 10:19-25.

THOUGHTS BY THE SPRING

*From his innermost being shall flow rivers of
living water.*

JOHN 7:38

When I was a child on our family's farm, one of my favorite places was the pond down by the barn. As a child, I always wondered where the water in the pond came from. I'd walk all the way around its edge but could never see any stream splashing into it. No waterfall. No pipes. What was flowing into the pond to make it so fresh and clear and full?

My dad patiently tried to explain that the pond was fed by a spring, a source of water from deep down in the earth. That spring, he told me, bubbled up from within and filled the little pond area. To me it was a big mystery.

I don't know how many times that little spring has come to my mind through the years...especially when I think about the Holy Spirit. We've all heard people say we should be filled with the Holy Spirit. Now, that's good, biblical counsel (Ephesians 5:18).

What kind of image does that create in your mind? How many of us picture the Spirit being poured into our lives from the *outside*...as if we were hollow mannequins? Just unscrew the cap on top of our heads, Lord, and fill us from the toes up! Do we get the idea that God's Spirit is being carried around in a massive pitcher, ready to be poured into us for the asking?

Yet, when the Bible talks about us being filled with the

Spirit, it's more accurate to picture a *spring*. When we obey God and yield our lives to Him, emptying ourselves of selfish desires, the Spirit of God is like a spring bubbling up within us...from down deep in our souls. The Spirit source fills us and we are satisfied. As Jesus said: "'He who believes in Me, as the Scripture said, "From his innermost being shall flow rivers of living water."' But this He spoke of the Spirit, whom those who believed in Him were to receive" (John 7:38-39).

If Dad had dug out a larger pond area in the dirt, that little spring would have continued to fill it. That might be good advice for you and me. If we would empty ourselves even further, letting go of our own rights, clearing out the debris of habitual sins, and humble ourselves further before the Lord, our *capacity* for God's Spirit would be increased.

He would fill us even more. And as our lives brim over from this ever-fresh wellspring within us, there will be plenty of refreshment for the thirsty souls of those around us.

STRONGHOLD

How would you describe the outflow from your life? A stream? A trickle? Take time with your Lord today to clear out any obstructions that might be hindering the spring within you.

THE LEAKY BUCKET

*Each of us should please his neighbor for his good,
to build him up.*

ROMANS 15:2, NIV

On the farm when we were kids, my sisters and I got involved in 4-H projects. One of those projects was raising calves. Oh boy, were they cute. I used to love to pet that silky, curly hair between their ears.

My sister had a milk formula which she had to mix and pour into a bucket—a bucket with a big nipple on the bottom for the calf to suck on. I remember one time when the only bucket I could find had a little hole in the bottom. The calf was bleating and crying for his dinner and there just wasn't another bucket around. I looked into the woeful face of that little calf and decided the only thing I could use was the leaky bucket.

First, I made certain to mix a lot of extra formula. Then I poured the measured amount into the leaky bucket. That little calf went for it, and while he kept on drinking, I kept pouring in as much—if not more—formula as I saw dripping out from the bottom. The calf got his dinner…as long as I was certain to pour it in faster than it trickled out.

That memory replayed in my mind recently when I heard a pastor talking about being filled with the Spirit. He was describing the despondency of so many Christians he counsels. Believers who find themselves filled with the Spirit one day and emptied out the next. They're frustrated and tired of getting drained-and-filled, drained-and-filled.

Those Christians, I reasoned, are simply leaky buckets. Welcome to the club! *All of us* are like leaky buckets, simply because we're human. And this whole cycle of getting drained and then filled up can be tiring if we try to go it alone.

The answer? It's simple. Make sure you've got somebody (or perhaps a great many somebodies) pouring their love and counsel and prayers into you faster than you find it leaking out. Fellowship. That's the solution. Brothers and sisters who will hold you accountable, study with you, sharpen you, and keep you on the straight path. Imperfect, "leaky" Christians who will pray for you as you pray for them.

Oh sure. You'll keep leaking…losing the zeal and fervor and excitement as you walk through life. This side of heaven it's inevitable. Just make sure you're part of a fellowship where you'll be filled up faster than you empty out. You might even find your "leaky" bucket overflowing into some of the empty buckets around you.

That's what being in the Body is all about.

STRONGHOLD

Take time to fill up on the advice of Romans 15:1-7. Will you commit yourself anew to pouring your love and counsel and prayers into a fellow believer trapped in the drain-and-fill cycle?

A BETTER JOY

Be glad because your names are written in heaven.
LUKE 10:20, GNB

hen Jesus chose seventy-two new disciples, it was the most exciting day any of the disciples could remember. Spiritual authority oozed from their pores. It was a heady experience, to say the least. "Lord, You just wouldn't believe it!" they exulted. "Even the demons took off when we spoke in Your name! It was great!"

Now, understandably, Jesus was thrilled for them and their new-found joy. He responded with genuine enthusiasm to the success of their ministry. Luke 10:21 says that He was "filled with joy." He burst into prayer and thanked His Father, praising Him that these men had tasted life the way it should be lived.

Yet at the same time, the Lord gently brought fresh focus to their gathering. Jesus said, "Don't be glad because the evil spirits obey you; rather be glad because your names are written in heaven" (Luke 10:20, GNB).

Can you identify with those seventy-two excited missionaries? Perhaps you've found yourself in a similar circumstance. You've been away for a week of fellowship with a group of exuberant believers. You've sat under the instruction of a first-rate Christian communicator, and you've come home a changed person. I mean, you've got joy! Your prayers seem to have more energy, you pray more specifically, with more faith. You even share Christ courageously and fearlessly—you're so excited!

You thought to yourself, "Oh, if we could only have it this way all of the time. If we could only have that speaker join our church. If we could only experience that sort of fellowship and prayer and excitement on a regular basis! Why does it have to end?"

I think the Lord would like to give us the same focus He gave to His disciples on that first, joyous day home from their journey. Don't let your joy depend on a lot of spiritual activities, highlights, and emotions. Don't let your gladness hinge on the next celestial lightning bolt or sun-splashed moment of meditation.

God wants our joy to rest on the simple fact that our names are written in heaven. There is no joy like the joy of our salvation! If Jesus Christ is your Savior and Lord, there is an entry on an actual page of an actual book in the highest heaven with YOUR NAME on it!

If *that* isn't enough to make you shout for joy, then you'd better close your prayer closet door behind you and find out why.

STRONGHOLD

Want to know more about that Book of Life which includes your name? Turn to Revelation 20:11-15 and then praise God that He always uses permanent ink! Have any doubt about that? For assurance, read Revelation 3:5.

EVERY GOOD GIFT

Every good and perfect gift is from above.

JAMES 1:17, NIV

Have you ever sat down with a pencil and pad to write out a "count your blessings" list? Maybe you've gotten as far as listing twenty items and thought you were done. After all, you had to stretch your thinking to be even *that* specific.

But there's more. So much more than we can possibly imagine. If we let the full impact of a verse like James 1:17 blow apart our old ideas about God's blessings, we'd see our list suddenly stretch past the horizon. James says every good time you have ever had in this world comes directly from God. (I mean *good* times—not sinful times.)

Can you think of the times you laughed and enjoyed yourself on an evening with friends? Can you remember the funny jokes?

Can you remember your first date? Well, maybe you'd like to forget the first date. How about your fifth date, when things got a bit more comfortable?

Can you remember hearing some music that went right to your heart and brought goose bumps to your back or tears to your eyes?

The Bible says here that your Father is the origin of every joyful smile that has ever crossed your face. Our God is the God of sunsets...and hot buttered popcorn...and red rosebuds...and spring rain...and Thanksgiving turkey…and bear hugs from your best friend…and freshly laundered towels…and ice tea on a hot summer day…and the laughter of a child.

Every good thing comes from the Father. Every single one. And more than that, those good things are *gifts*. Gifts to be received with heartfelt gratitude.

All too often, though, you and I save our mental checklists for all the bad and discouraging things—all the times we've ever been disappointed, embarrassed, used, humiliated, or hurt. And soon we find ourselves irritated and complaining—clutched at the throat by an ungrateful spirit.

Even though our own pain might scream for our undivided attention, God wants us to come to Him with a heart full of thankfulness for all the good things in this life. Everything from the joy of a Christ-centered friendship to the first lick of a Baskin-Robbins pistachio ice cream cone.

Every good gift comes from the same Giver.

STRONGHOLD

"Count Your Blessings!" You've probably sung this old hymn (or heard it sung) scores of times. Now is the time to sing it afresh. And remember…sing it with gusto. After all, you've got a lot of good gifts to thank God for!

THOUGHTS ON A CLEAR DAY

He is the faithful God.
DEUTERONOMY 7:9, NIV

The morning broke crisp and clear, electric with excitement. Several days had passed with hardly a problem...no inconveniences, no last-minute pressures, no disagreements with my husband. Nothing but clear sailing.

I was on my way to work, looking forward to digging into the day's duties. Right out loud in my van I exclaimed, "Oh, Lord, You're just so good! You're really a wonderful God." And I meant it. God is good—and wonderful beyond telling.

But...why is it that we are most *certain* of His goodness when things are going smoothly? When the weather invigorates us, when the bills are all paid, when the medical check-up goes just fine, when no problems plague us and no hassles hound us. Praise at those times comes so easily.

You and I are prone to let our *circumstances*—whether good or bad—dictate our view of God. If things are great, then God is good. If we feel threatened or anxious, then God must be off somewhere, watching over the saints in Australia or answering some grandmother's prayer in Iceland.

Needless to say, it shouldn't be that way...and you and I know it. Time and time again the Bible tells us that God is faithful.

Moses wanted there to be no doubt. "Know therefore that the LORD your God is God," he told his people. *"He is the faithful God,* keeping his covenant of love to a thousand generations of those who love him" (Deuteronomy 7:9, NIV).

The apostle John underlined the truth in a way we can never forget. "If we confess our sins, *he is faithful and just* and will forgive us our sins and purify us from all unrighteousness" (1 John 1:9, NIV).

The writer of Hebrews urges us to "hold unswervingly to the hope we profess, for *he who promised is faithful"* (Hebrews 10:23, NIV).

Psalm 146:6 assures us that the Lord r*emains faithful forever.*

Paul signs off a letter to Thessalonica with the reminder that *"the one who calls you is faithful* and he will do it" (1 Thessalonians 5:24, NIV).

Scripture, and Scripture alone, should be our frame of reference for who God really is. Scripture tells us that *every* day is a great day to give praise to God.

STRONGHOLD

You think your circumstances are bad! Look at 2 Kings 25:1-12 to see what God's people faced during the Babylonian invasion of Jerusalem. Now, read Jeremiah's assessment of those circumstances in Lamentations 3:21-25. Can you pray Jeremiah's beautiful prayer in Lamentations 3 today as you consider your own circumstances, good or bad?

A KINGDOM UNSHAKEN

We are receiving a kingdom that cannot be shaken.

HEBREWS 12:28, NIV

I t was the middle of the night, and the first thing I heard was the windows rattling. Then everything in the room started to sway.

Usually a solid sleeper, even Ken woke.

"Ken, that was an earthquake, wasn't it?"

"Yeah," he replied, "and a pretty big one, too." Then he rolled over and went back to sleep! No big deal, I guess, for a California native.

But that was not the case for me. This Maryland girl lay awake for hours. What a strange, helpless feeling it had been—not knowing how long or how hard the earth was going to shake. What if it had been..."the big one"? Would our roof collapse? Where would we turn off the gas? Were we ready with stored up food and water?

Oh, the questionings and imaginings that can go through my mind in the middle of the night—especially when I'm the only one awake.

It wasn't long, though, before those panicky thoughts gave way to a still, persistent voice speaking from a room inside my heart. How long had the voice been speaking—since the earthquake began? The Lord comforted me with a verse we had just studied in our women's Bible study a couple weeks before. "Therefore, since we are receiving a kingdom that cannot be shaken, let us be thankful, and so worship God acceptably with reverence and awe" (Hebrews 12:28, NIV).

Now that's a verse that fit the need of the moment! The earthquake was God's audio-visual aid to me that the solid rock-bottom things we tend to depend on—like the earth, for instance—could be here today and gone tomorrow.

We live in a world that is terrified of a sliding Dow Jones Average and a rising Richter Scale…of falling missiles and a climbing cancer rate.

Let's praise God for a future that can never be shaken.

No matter what.

STRONGHOLD

Here in southern California you'll hardly ever find newly built homes made of brick because bricks crumble in earthquakes. What kind of "home" are you building? Read Matthew 7:24-29 for a good master-building plan.

MEMORIES

I thank my God every time I remember you.
PHILIPPIANS 1:3, NIV

emories, pressed between the pages of my mind, memories, sweetened through the ages just like wine."[4] I like that song. And even though it's a contemporary tune, it could well have been penned by a lonely apostle named Paul, passing the long hours in a dark Roman dungeon.

Cut off from fresh air, sunlight, and—most of all—companionship, Paul was warmed by memories of his friends, the Philippians. Closing his eyes, he could see their faces, hear their voices, feel their warm embrace.

So it is during life's longest, darkest hours. In lonely intervals away from our family...in an extended stay in a hospital...in an overseas assignment that seems to stretch on and on...in the vacant room once filled with the presence of a loved one. At times and places such as these, light-filled memories can help fill the emptiness and ease the ache of loneliness.

Today, as I write these words, marks the seventeenth anniversary of that hot summer day when I broke my neck—and altered the whole course of my life. I was seventeen on that day when I dove into the shallow waters of the Chesapeake, so I've now spent as many years in a wheelchair as on my feet. It's been a long journey...yes, and a difficult one.

Yet nice memories have a way of buoying my spirits. I treasure some of those memories. Like the sensation of walking on the warm concrete apron of a swimming pool. Or the feel of wet leather reins in my hands. Or even drumming my fingers on a desk. Kind of a funny feeling, especially if my nails were long.

Those might not sound like much to you, but to me they represent warm and sunlit moments of my past.

So on this seventeenth anniversary of my injury I say, "Thank you, God, for the wonderful things I can still remember. Thank you that these memories help me to appreciate how precious our health really is. Oh, and help me, Lord, not to take for granted those things I can feel and do and experience. And Father...may the next seventeen years be as rewarding and enriching as what I've experienced so far. Let me keep making memories, memories to savor for years to come."

STRONGHOLD

What kind of memories did Paul have of Philippi? Turn to Acts 16:11-15 and 16:25-40. What thrilling reminders of God's marvelous works helped Paul in his loneliness?

CHOOSING YOUR ATTITUDE TOWARD WORK

As slaves of Christ, doing the will of God from the heart.
EPHESIANS 6:6

A friend and I were talking recently about the attitudes Christians hold toward their jobs—whether inside or outside the home. "It's Ephesians 6:6 that goes right to the heart of it, Joni," my friend told me. "Paul says that we shouldn't go about our tasks in order to please men, but as slaves of Christ, doing the will of God from the heart."

I immediately thought of Joseph. If there was ever anybody who did his best at a job in order to do God's will from the heart, it was this young teenager in the book of Genesis.

Loved and trusted by his father, Joseph was probably the most conscientious shepherd in the whole family. In fact, he did such a good job of shepherding that his jealous brothers sold him into slavery.

So what did Joseph do then? He became the best slave he could possibly become. He was such an honest, honorable slave that he chose faithfulness to his master rather than playing games with his master's wife. He was rewarded by being thrown into prison.

Then he concentrated on becoming a model prisoner—the best in all of Egypt. And how was he repaid? He was forgotten by the very ones who should have remembered his faithful service and he remained imprisoned for two long years.

Joseph's journey from shepherd to slave to prisoner is ironic. He was so sincere. So obedient. *We* would expect his lot to get lighter as he went along. But should a *servant* expect that? Isn't it a servant's duty to do his master's bidding, whatever the task? Overall, God seemed less concerned with Joseph's release and relief and more concerned with seasoning his character.

The day came, however, when God decided his man was ready. In a single hour, Joseph went from a corner in the dungeon to the right hand of Pharaoh. From a lifer in the federal pen to the Secretary of the Treasury.

What's remarkable is that none of those years spent as a slave or prisoner were wasted. God had neither forgotten him nor lost track of his situation. The discipline and endurance and patience and obedience were all needed to mold Joseph for a key role in his generation.

Wherever we find ourselves today, let's take a little encouragement from Joseph. No matter how lofty or lowly the role He has given us to play in this old world, He simply asks us to do His will.

STRONGHOLD

The entire second chapter of Philippians reads like an attitude check-list. Read verses 5-11 and take a check-up!

ENCORES

Do not dwell on the past.

ISAIAH 43:18, NIV

Have you ever been so moved by the music at a concert you found yourself wishing that "last song" would never come? When it finally came, what did you do? You probably jumped to your feet, applauding wildly, and called for an encore. What an exhilarating feeling to see that entertainer come back out on stage, pick up the mike, and launch into one more song.

Encores. They give you the illusion of squeezing one more measure of light and joy and goose bumps out of a happy circumstance.

Do you remember a special weekend retreat with a bunch of Christians? The close, friendly feelings were like nothing you'd experienced before. The speaker was on target. The spiritual atmosphere seemed supercharged. Unsaved friends came to know the Lord. Christians got their lives back on track.

Didn't you feel like asking God for an encore? With those memories fresh in your mind, didn't you feel like imploring God for more of the same?

Well, you know what? He won't do it. God doesn't give encores. Psalm 62:11 tells that "one thing God has spoken"(NIV). The Lord states it even more forcefully in the book of Isaiah. "Forget the former things; do not dwell on the past. See, I am doing a new thing! Now it springs up; do you not perceive it?" (43:18-19, NIV).

God will never do the same thing exactly the same way a second time around. But He will do something better. He will perform something new, something different, that is just as special, just as significant as any of your most memorable moments with Him.

So how about it? Are you looking forward to an upcoming get-together with a few other Christians? A retreat perhaps? A Bible study? Are you in the middle of plans for an annual event and you're wringing your hands, hoping and praying it will turn out like "last year"?

Don't let your prayers get mediocre! Don't ask God for something He did last year. Don't simply expect Him to do an encore. Don't dwell on "the former things."

But do expect Him to speak. Remember, this is the God who is "able to do immeasurably more than all we ask or imagine, according to his power that is at work within us" (Ephesians 3:20, NIV). So stretch your faith and believe Him for something far greater than a simple encore.

He's ready to do "a new thing" in your life...today.

STRONGHOLD

Read Isaiah 48:3-8 to see what God said to a bunch of Israelites who were tired of the way God works. By contrast read Hebrews 10:19-25 for the writer's glimpse of a "new and living way" shown by Jesus.

HOPE ON TIPTOE

The whole creation is on tiptoe to see the wonderful sight of the sons of God coming into their own.

ROMANS 8:19, PHILLIPS

etting out into nature is serious business for the Tadas. This is one Maryland flower that begins to wilt if she can't escape the confines of Los Angeles now and then for short forays among God's handiwork.

It could be desert camping in the Mojave in the early spring. Or a short drive along the Los Angeles Crest Highway, which tops the San Gabriel mountains and offers vistas of craggy peaks and Ponderosa pines. Or a Saturday afternoon parked on some cliff, watching the sea gulls swirl and swoop along the crest of the breakers.

Yes, nature is personal to me. And—did you know? Nature even has its own personal verse in Scripture. Romans 8:19 tells us that "The whole creation is on tiptoe to see the wonderful sight of the sons of God coming into their own" (Phillips).

On tiptoe. In some mysterious way, the flowers and plants and animals and seascapes and landscapes wait in eager expectation for…a glory yet to be revealed.

Paul tells a little more about this anticipation in verses 20-21. The creation is groaning and longing for the day when God will release it from its bondage and usher in a new era with Christ as King. Can you hear the sighing in the wind? Can you feel the heavy silence in the mountains? Can you sense the restless longing in the sea? Something's coming...something better.

But consider this: If the whole inanimate and brute creation has an earnest expectation, surely we believers—the sons and daughters of God—should have nothing less!

How's your hope today? Do you find yourself longing and looking forward to the glorious appearing of the Lord Jesus Christ?

If nature waits on tiptoe for the coming of Jesus, you and I shouldn't be caught flat-footed!

STRONGHOLD

Chuck Swindoll urges believers to meditate on passages such as 1 Thessalonians 4:13-18—verses that describe the day when Jesus Christ will return to earth. "Talk about high drama!" he writes. "Remind yourself that this experience could happen at any moment—even before you return from your walk...or draw your next breath." [5]

5. Charles R. Swindoll, *Growing Deep in the Christian Life* (Portland, Ore.: Multnomah Press, 1986), p. 280.

A SPARROW MAKES THE POINT

So don't be afraid.
MATTHEW 10:31, NIV

I was just a little girl when my mom and dad took me to the Baltimore Zoo. But there is one part of that visit I will never forget.

For some reason, the aviary seized my attention more than the elephants, monkeys, and giraffes put together. A large bird exhibition, it was aflutter with fascinating feathered creatures…brightly colored parrots, funny-looking toucans, huge, stern eagles, and know-it-all owls. But flittering around the outside of all the cages were common sparrows, making their homes in the rafters of the aviary.

They weren't important enough to put in a cage for everyone to admire and ogle. They didn't rate an explanatory plaque. Their pictures didn't appear in the zoo guidebook. Mostly, they weren't even noticed.

Yet of all the birds He created, God chose the sparrow to make a crucial point on the subject of fear. Jesus knows how vulnerable we feel at times. How weak mentally, how frail emotionally. A surprising number of us let our apprehensions press us to the edge of our mental limits every once in a while.

Just recently I was there. That's when I came across our Lord's little lecture on sparrows. Jesus was speaking to His men about future events. When He read the fear rising in their hearts, He paused to reassure them. "Are not two sparrows sold for a penny? Yet not one of them will fall to the ground apart from the will of your Father. And even the very hairs of your head are all numbered. So don't be afraid; you are worth more than many sparrows" (Matthew 10:29-31, NIV).

How wise of our Lord to use the example of a sparrow! He could have used eagles. Or hawks, or falcons, or wide-winged storks. Yet out of the world's nine thousand bird species, the Lord chose one of the most insignificant, least noticed birds flying around. A scruffy little sparrow.

Jesus obviously wanted to make His point clear. Those who believe and follow Him mean more to the Father than anything else. If God takes note of each humble sparrow, where they are and what they're doing, you'd better believe He keeps tabs on you.

"Do not be afraid, little flock," Jesus tells us, "for your Father has been pleased to give you the kingdom" (Luke 12:32, NIV).

So why be anxious? Why be assaulted by fears? Why be pressed with worry and doubt? If the great God of Heaven concerns Himself with the little sparrow clinging to a twig outside your window, He cares about what concerns you.

Stronghold

Read Psalm 55:22 and then 1 Peter 5:7. Pour out your anxieties before Him today. You've nothing to lose but your fear.

FRAME OF REFERENCE

In Him all things hold together.
COLOSSIANS 1:17

There are no hard and fast rules about jigsaw puzzles. All of us have our own system. But when Ken and I clear off one end of the kitchen table on a lazy Sunday afternoon and go to work on one of those 600-piece beauties, experience has taught us to begin with the edge of the picture.

Before you cement the edges together, it's an impossible jumble of colors, curves, and irreconcilable fragments. But after you get the boundaries staked out, everything seems to have a context.

It struck me recently that working on a jigsaw puzzle isn't all that different from working on our Christian walk. I like to think of God's truth in Scripture as pieces of some grand puzzle. And the frame...the most important part...is Jesus. Start there. Begin with the Gospels. Learn what He thinks about your sin. Observe His love. Study His conversations. Memorize His words. Learn how He went to the cross and died for you. Rejoice in the resurrection. All these things are like a gigantic frame. The Lord Jesus is like the completed edge around the picture of your life.

On the Emmaus road, the resurrected Jesus Christ walked and talked with two grieving disciples. At that point, they didn't recognize their Lord. So they spilled their frustration and sorrow into the ears of the Stranger who walked in their midst. Now that Jesus had been crucified, what was going to come of the promises in Scripture that Messiah would redeem His people?

What did Jesus do? He took them to the Frame. "And beginning with Moses and with all the prophets, He explained to them the things concerning Himself in all the Scriptures." And then "their eyes were opened and they recognized Him" (Luke 24:27, 31).

Jesus is the Frame of Reference that draws all of Scripture together into one grand design, one complete picture. All that we learn in Scripture relates to Him.

Puzzling today over the odd-shaped, varicolored fragments of your life? Need a frame of reference?

Take a peek at the picture on the puzzle box. It's a portrait of Jesus.

STRONGHOLD

In John 5:16-47, Jesus had a talk with some religious leaders who got hung up on a few of the puzzle pieces of Scripture. They were ignoring the frame. Take time to read those verses, zeroing in on verses 39-40, and see what Jesus has to say about the completed picture of the puzzle.

JOB'S WIFE

*If when you do what is right and suffer for it you
patiently endure it, this finds favor with God.*

1 PETER 2:20

Which of us hasn't read, or at least heard, of the story of Job? Countless books and Bible commentaries have been penned about this man and his avalanche of adversity. Oh sure, he voiced his share of complaints and wrestled with more than a few doubts. But not once did he curse God. Even after he learned of the terrible destruction which ripped through his family, his possessions, and his servants, he praised the Lord.

Yes, Job went through a lot, but have you ever stopped to think about Job's wife? When it comes right down to it, his wife went through just as much as he did. She also felt the crushing loss of her sons and daughters. She also lost her possessions and cherished household servants. And what's more, she had to stand by and watch as her husband—the only one left of her family— suffered indescribable pain and sorrow. Only someone who has experienced the helpless anxiety of watching a loved one suffer can identify with that hurt.

There may be good reasons why Job's wife doesn't hold an honored place in history. One glance at Scripture tells us she had anything but the patience of her husband. She sees her life falling to pieces around her, all her secure props knocked out from underneath her. She sees her husband driven to the point of despair. And what does she do? Her first piece of advice is recorded in Job 2:9: "Are you still trying to be godly when God has done all this to you? Curse him and die" (TLB).

You get the impression that she's as angry with her husband as she is with God! Whatever her wedding vows may have been, she evidently ignored the portions that said, "For better or for worse, for richer or for poorer, in sickness and in health." Blinded by her own misery and despair, she could only lash out in anger and bitterness.

My heart goes out to her. Few of us will ever be touched by that kind of grief and loss. And what one of us can really be sure of how we would respond if all of those things happened to us?

It would be a good idea to think about a response before a major trial or testing descends upon our life. How, by God's grace, would we respond...to Him...to our loved ones?

Patience, the apostle Paul tells us, is a gift from God. A gift that the Holy Spirit supernaturally produces as we daily yield our lives (even the little things) to His control.

STRONGHOLD

Read Habakkuk 3:17-18. Are you enjoying a time of safety, good health, and happiness? List your favorite people and possessions and commit them to God right now.